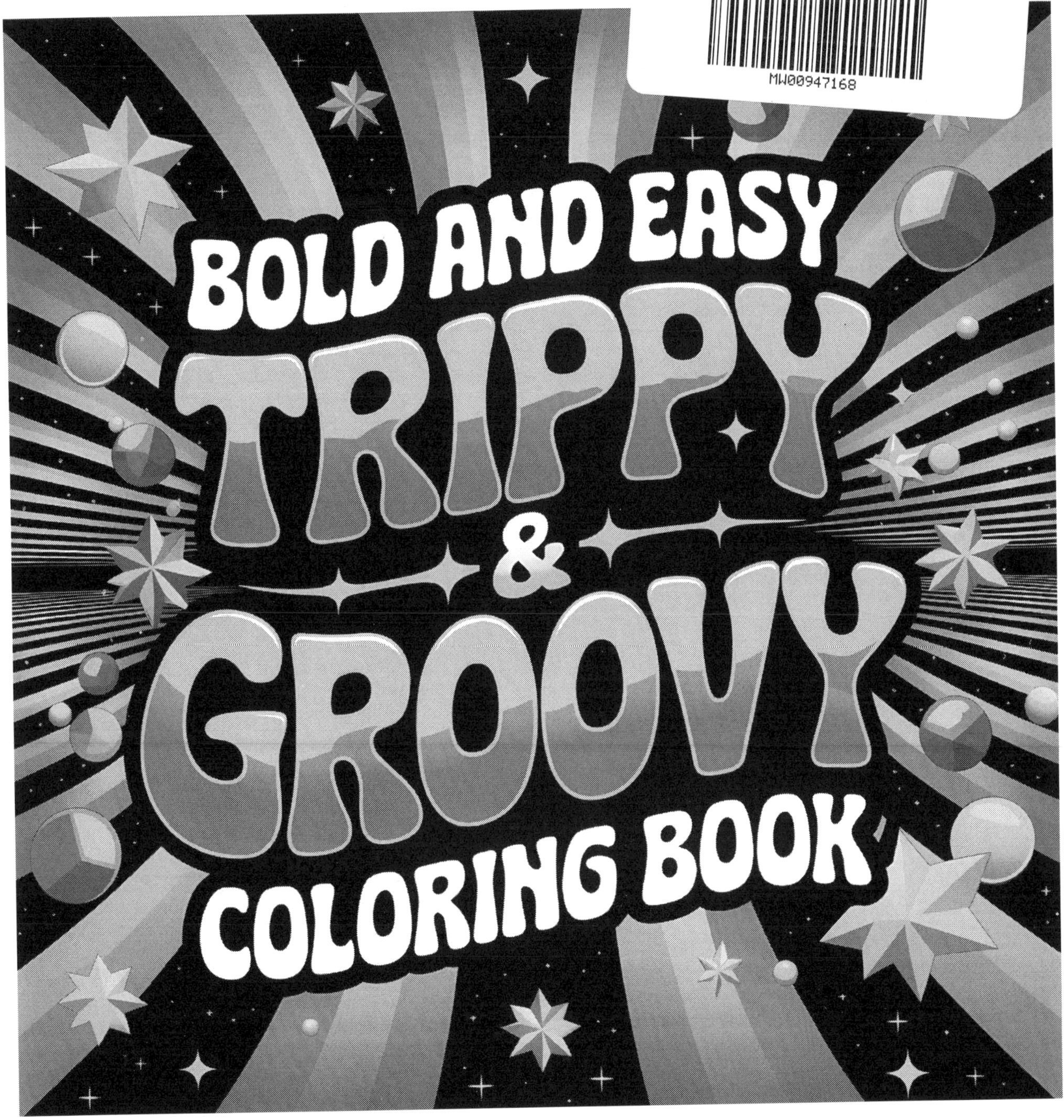

MW00947168

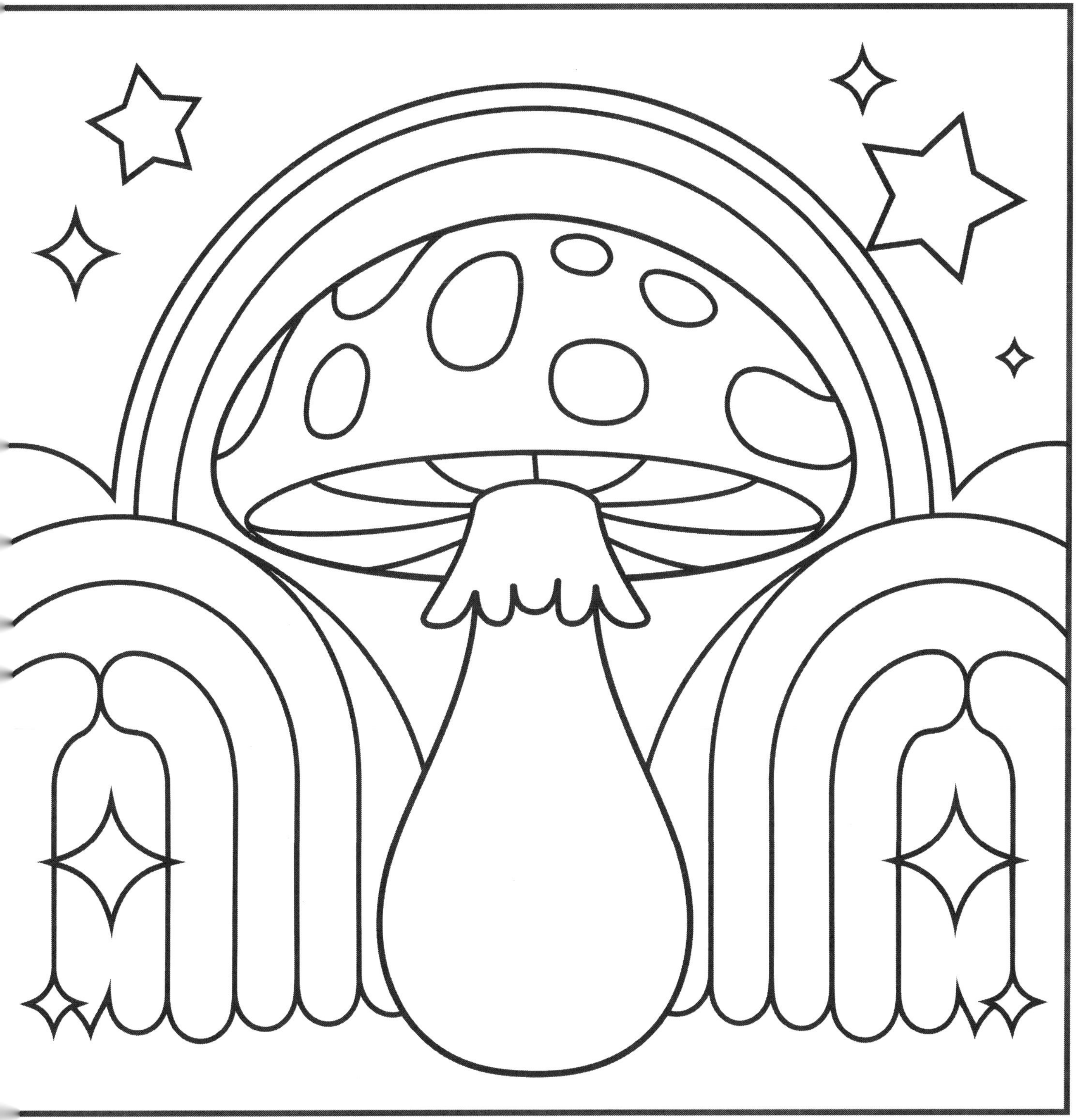

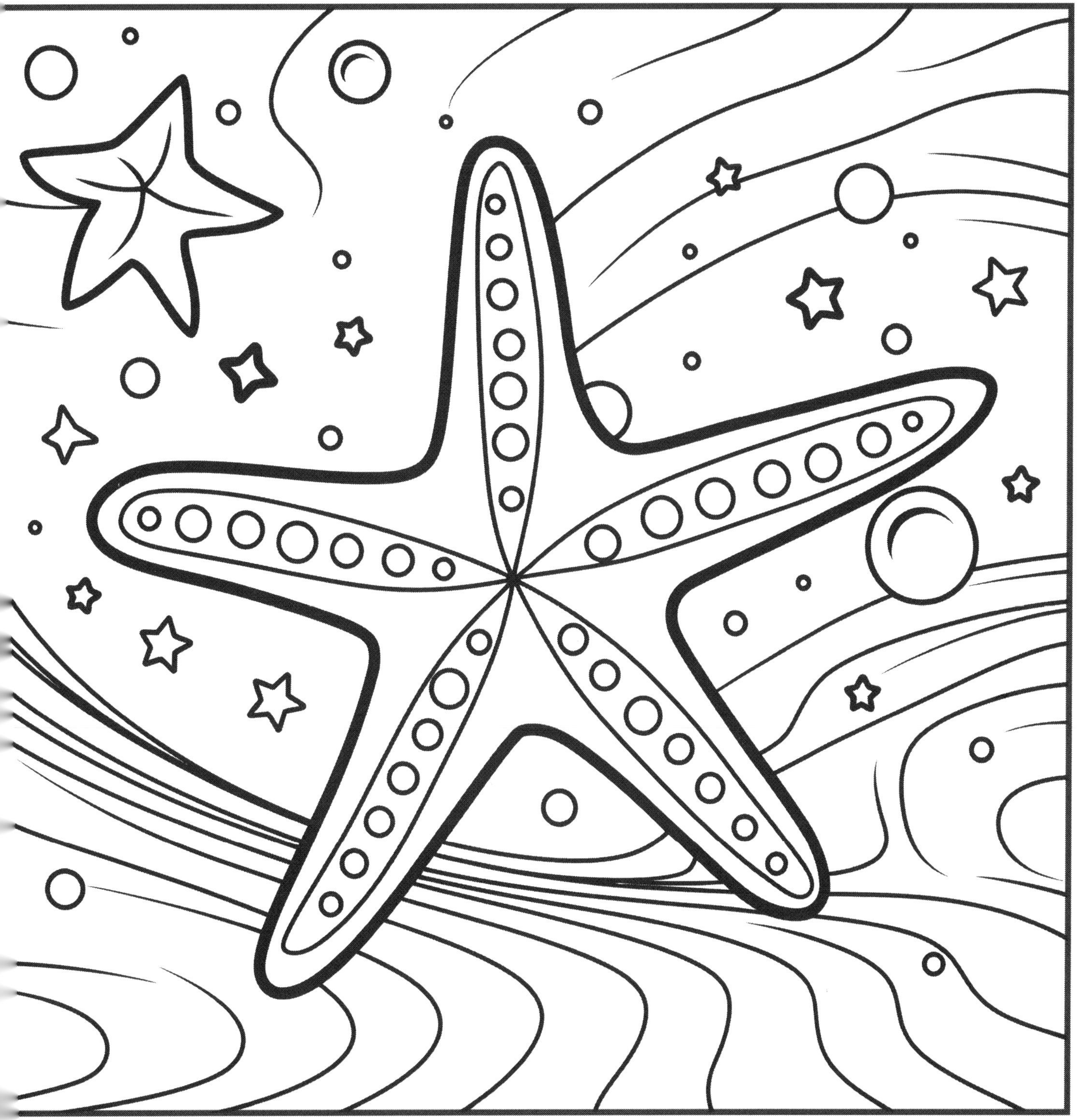

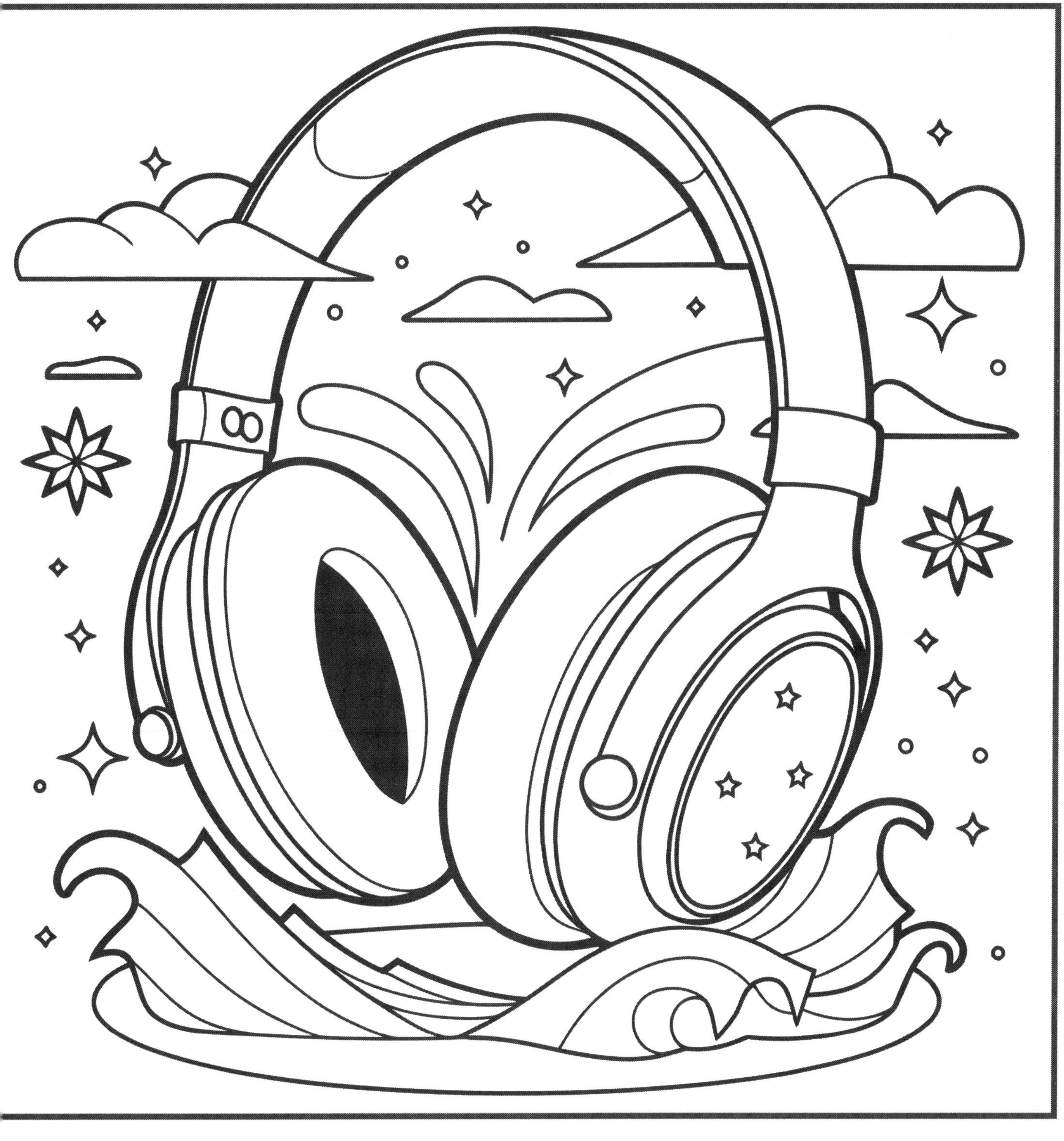

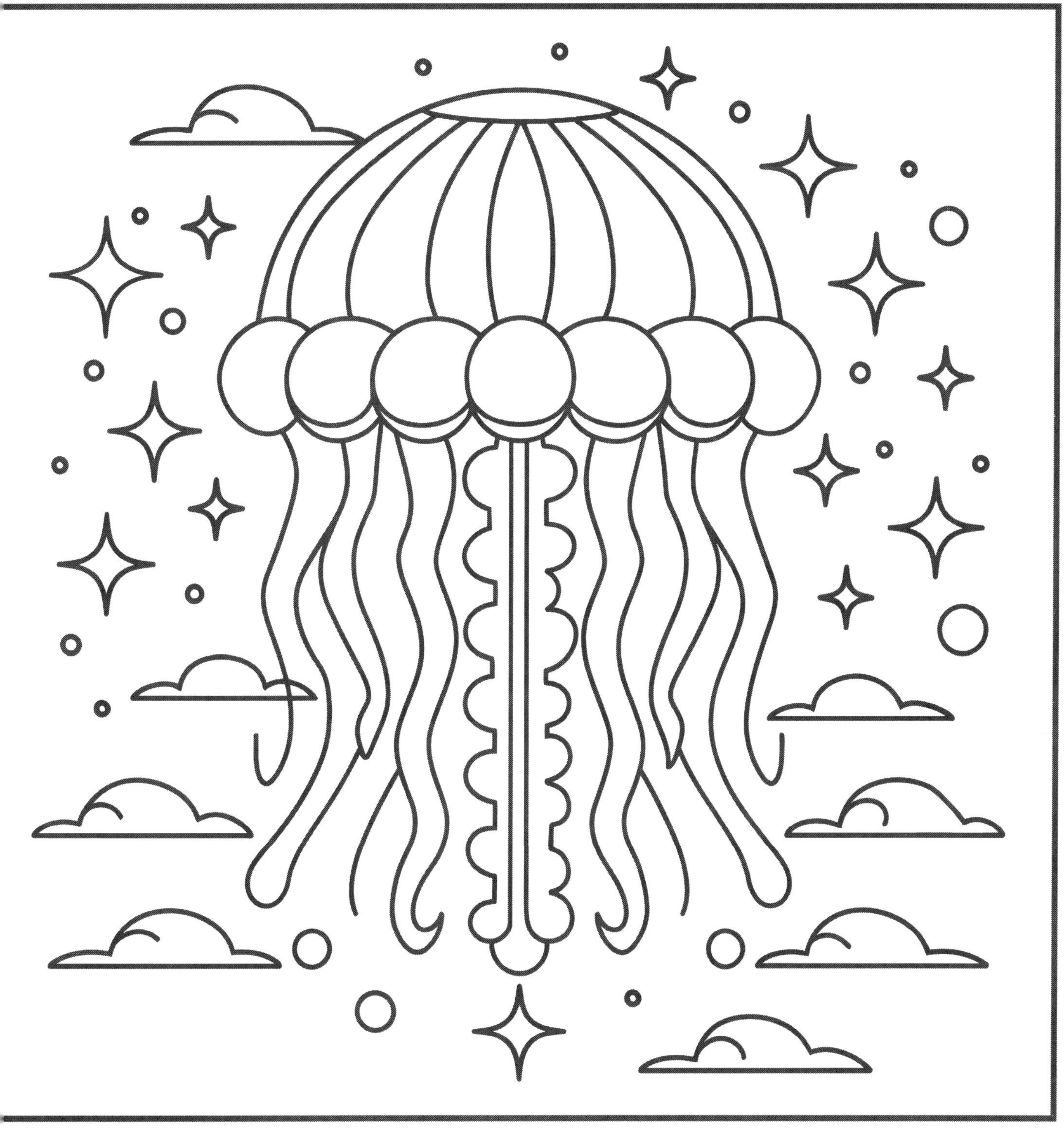

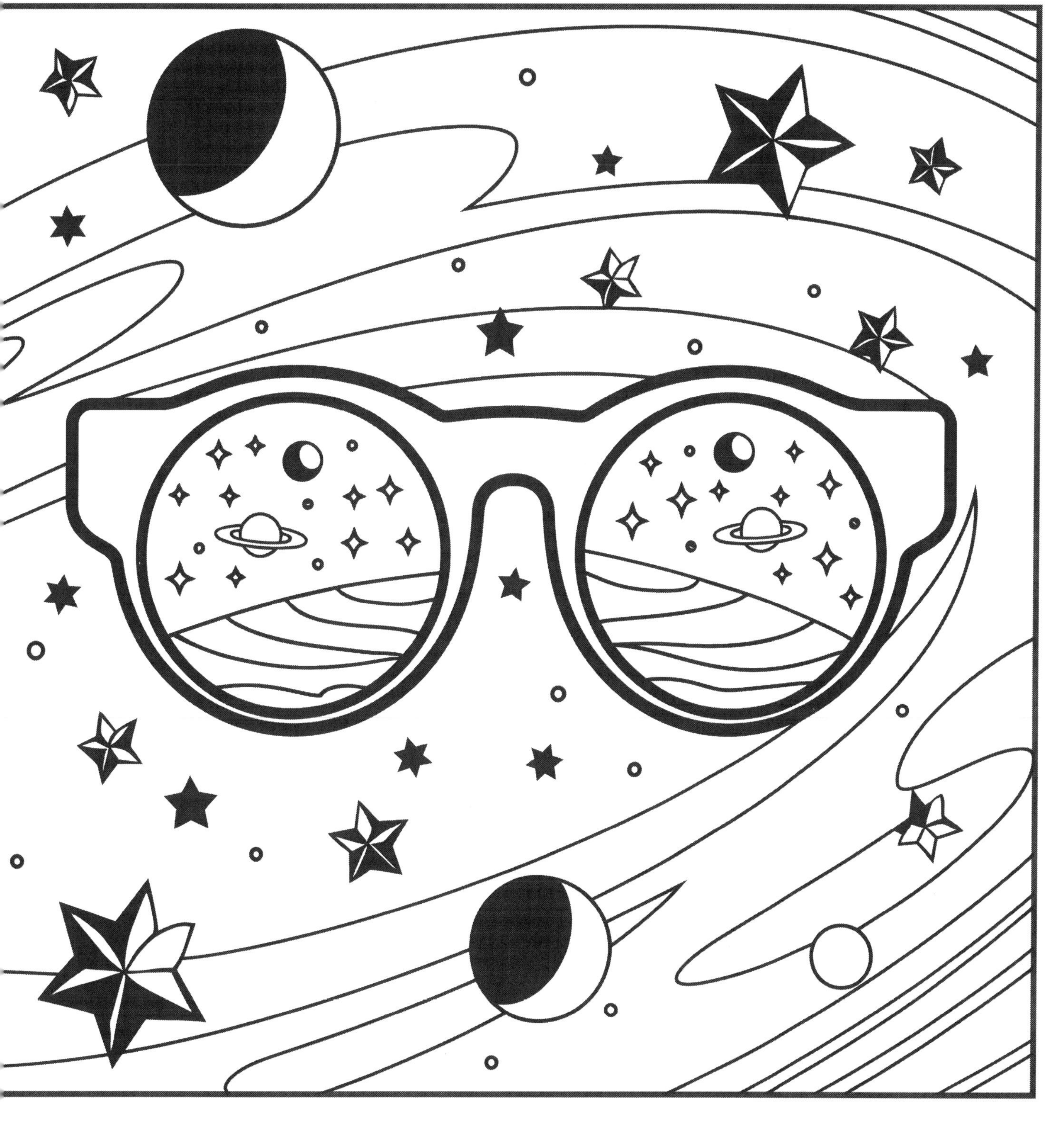

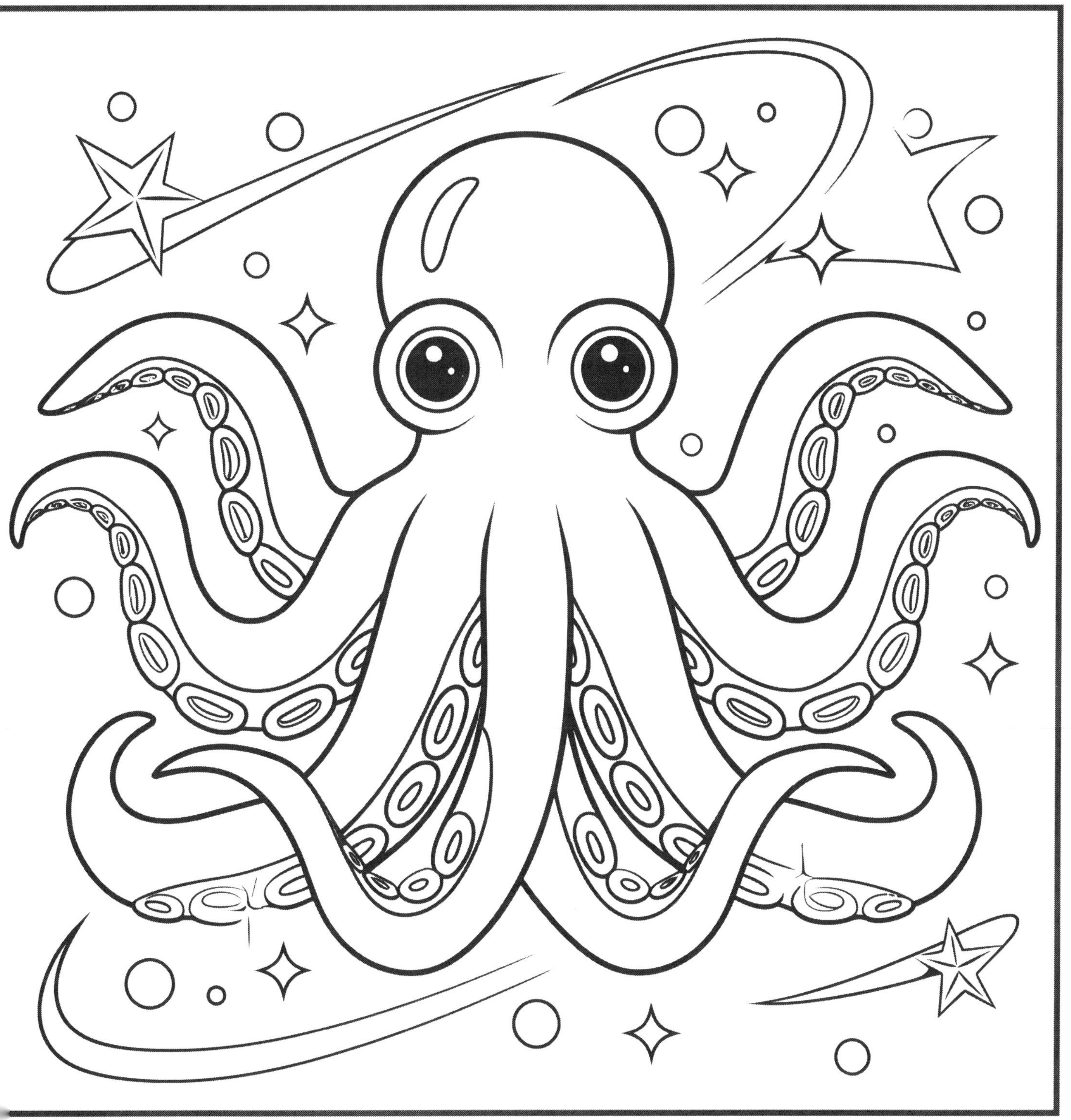

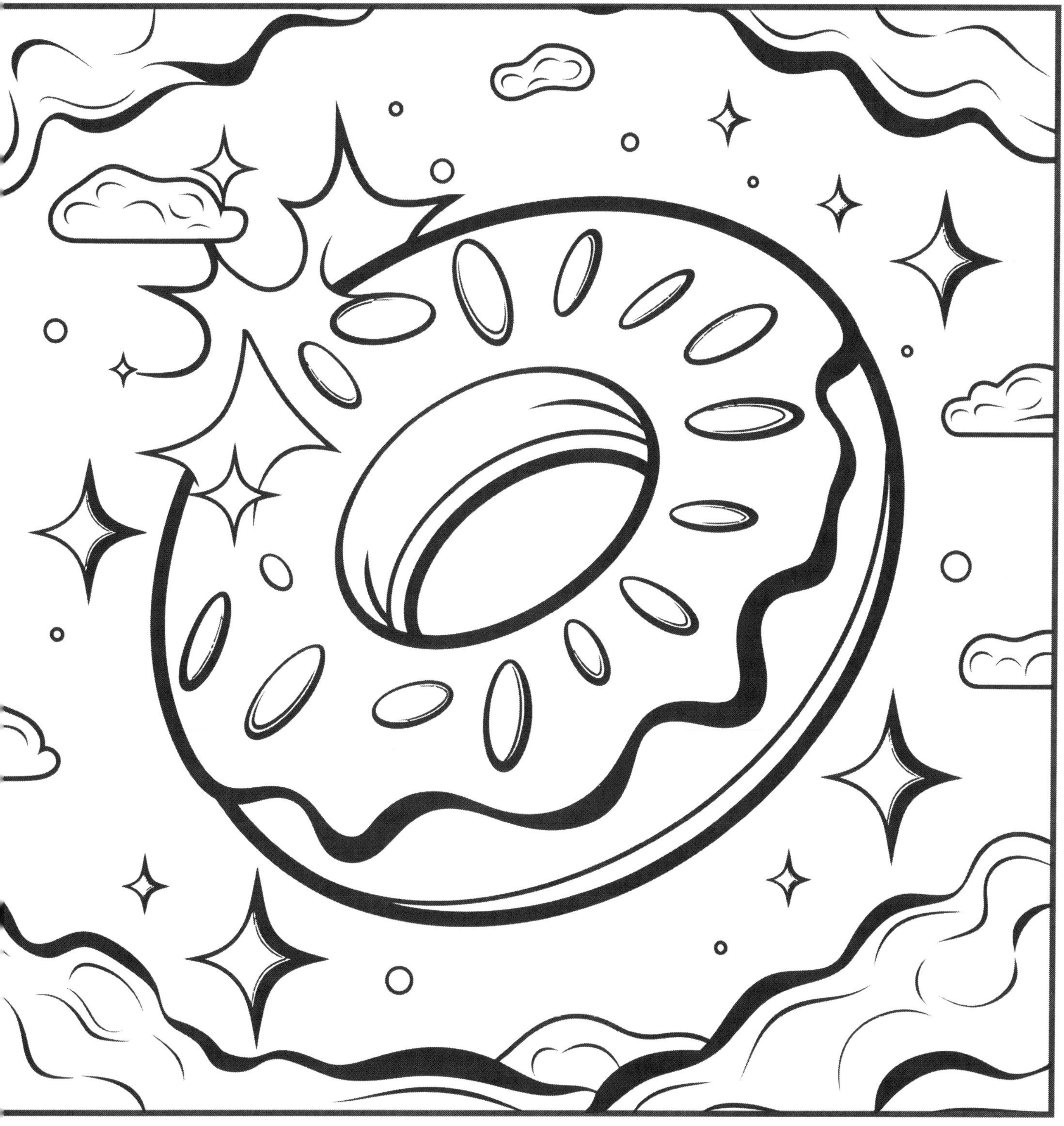

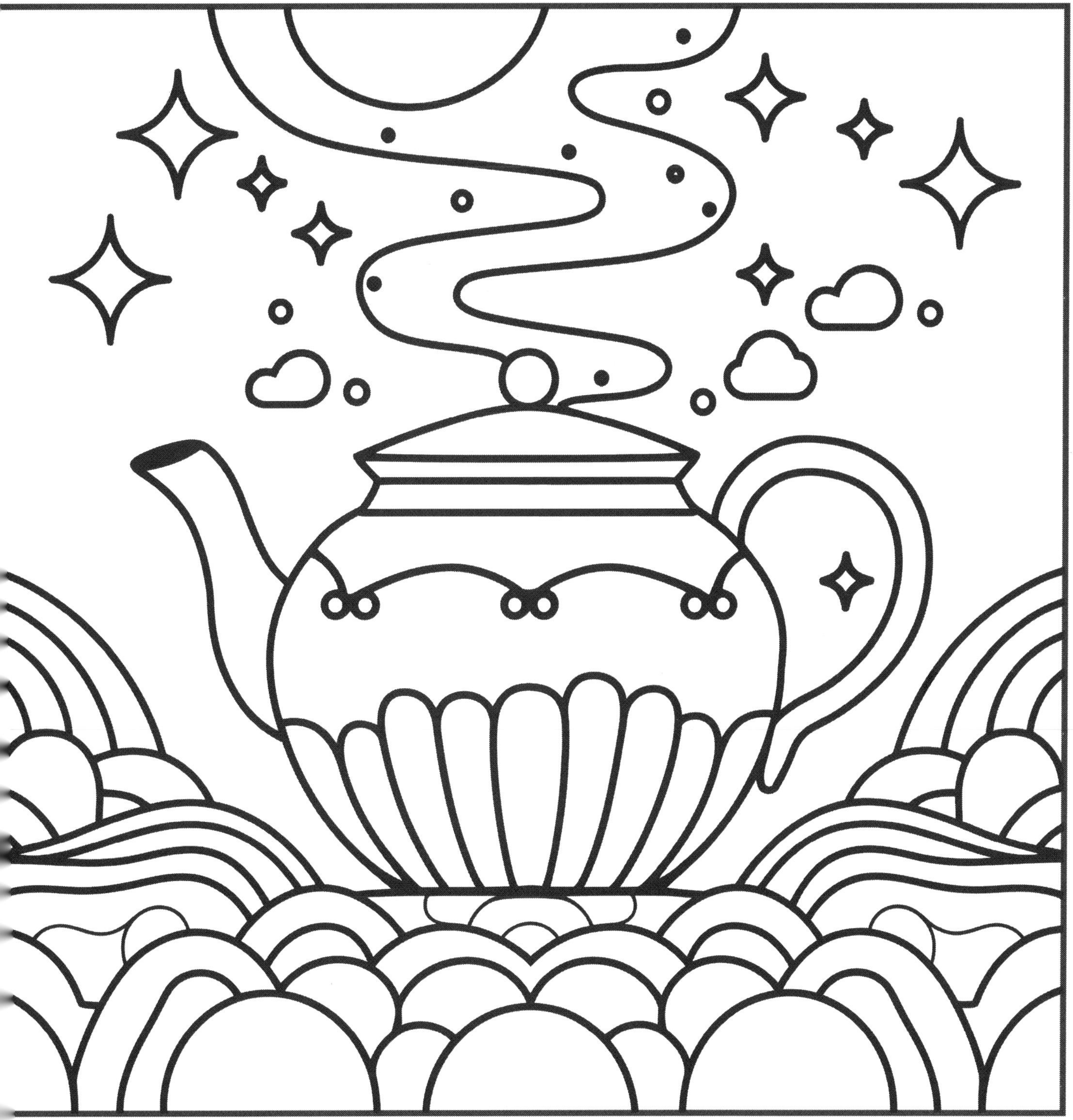

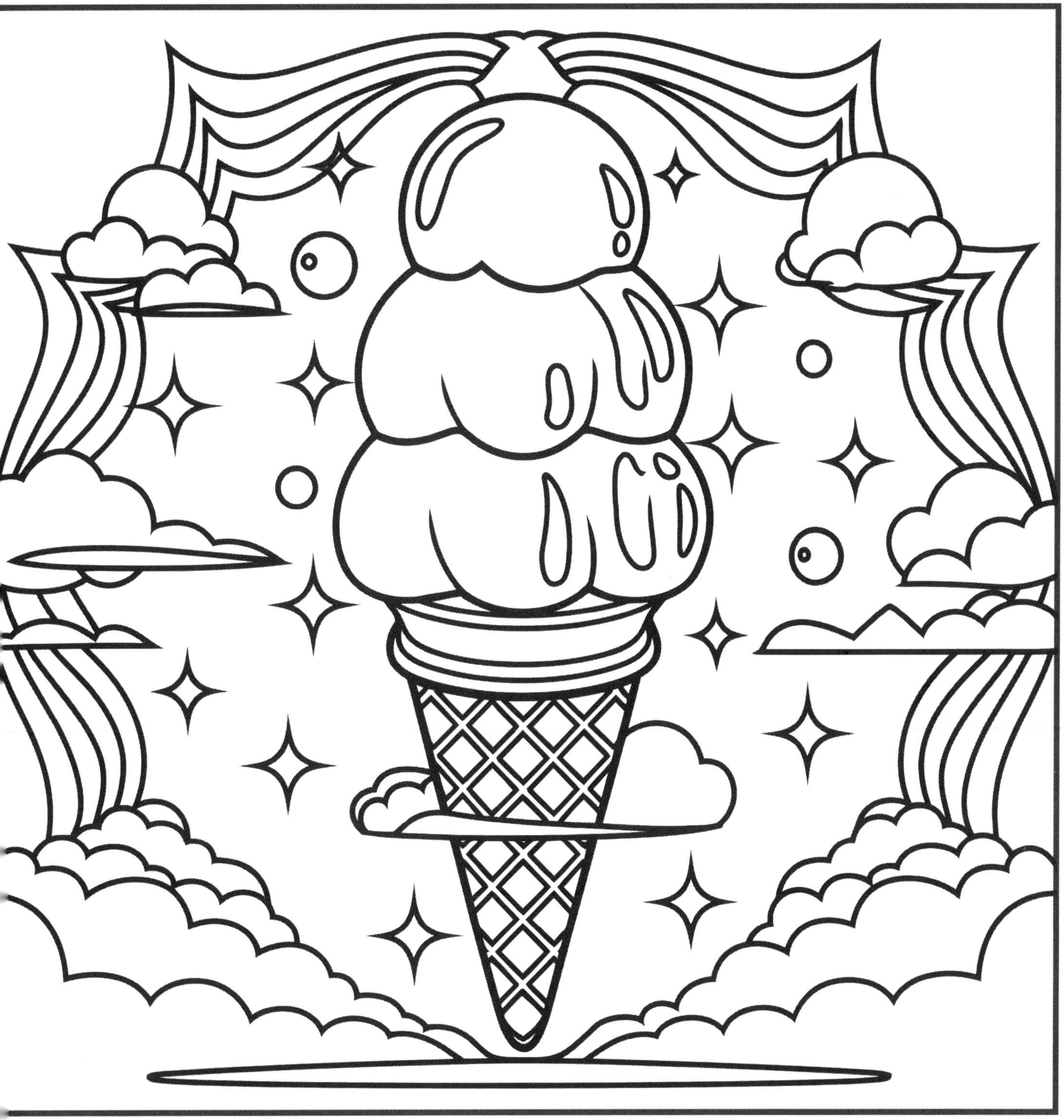

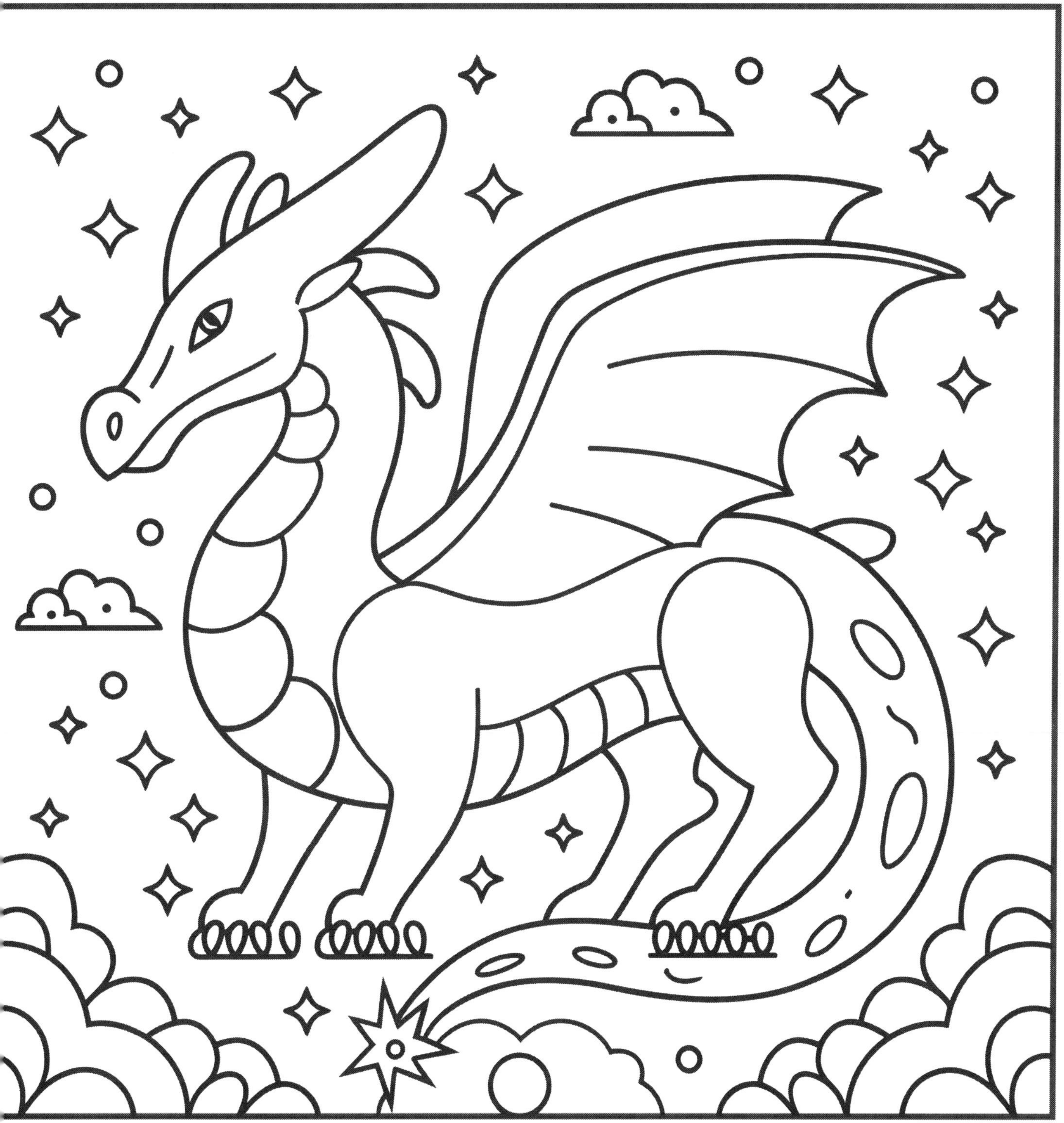

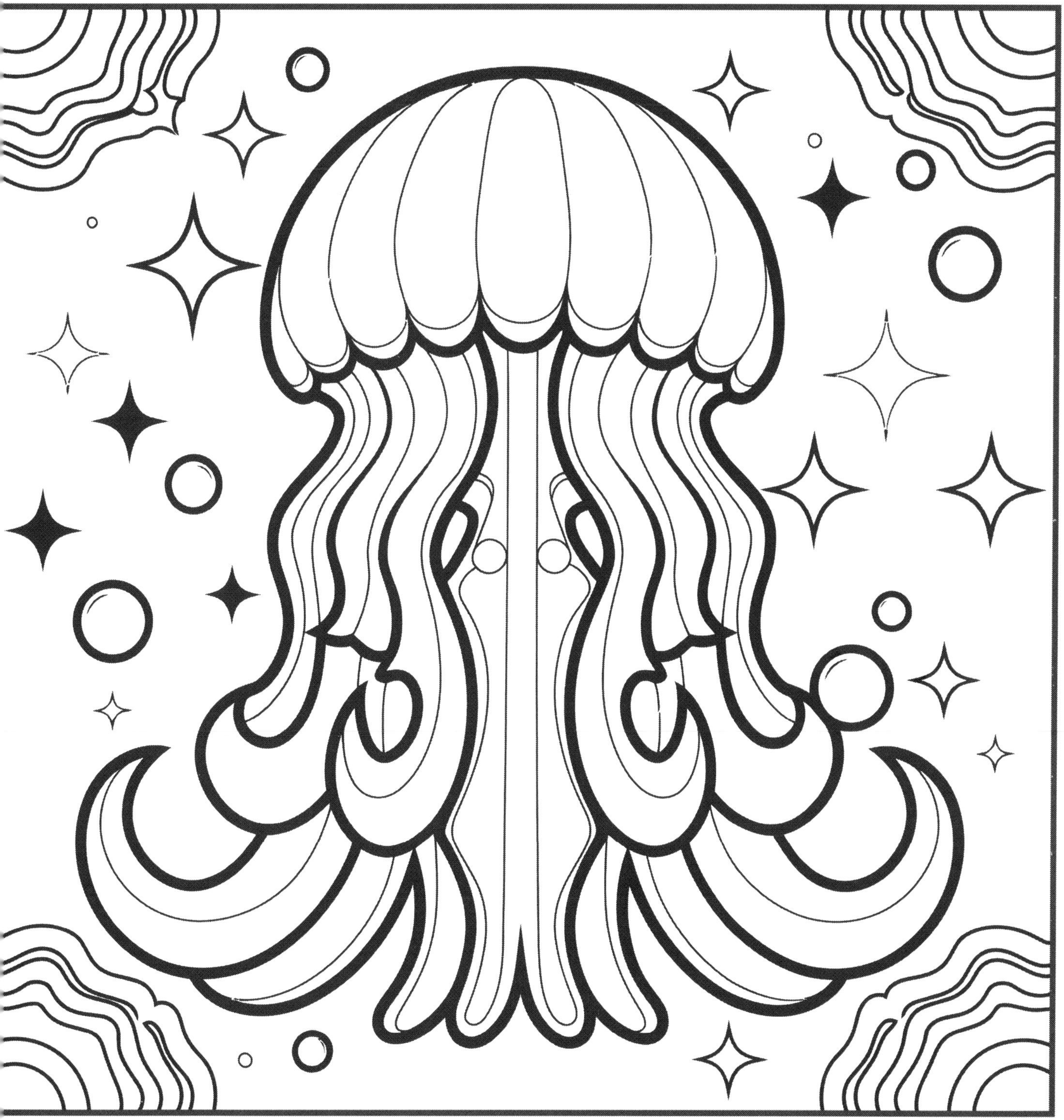

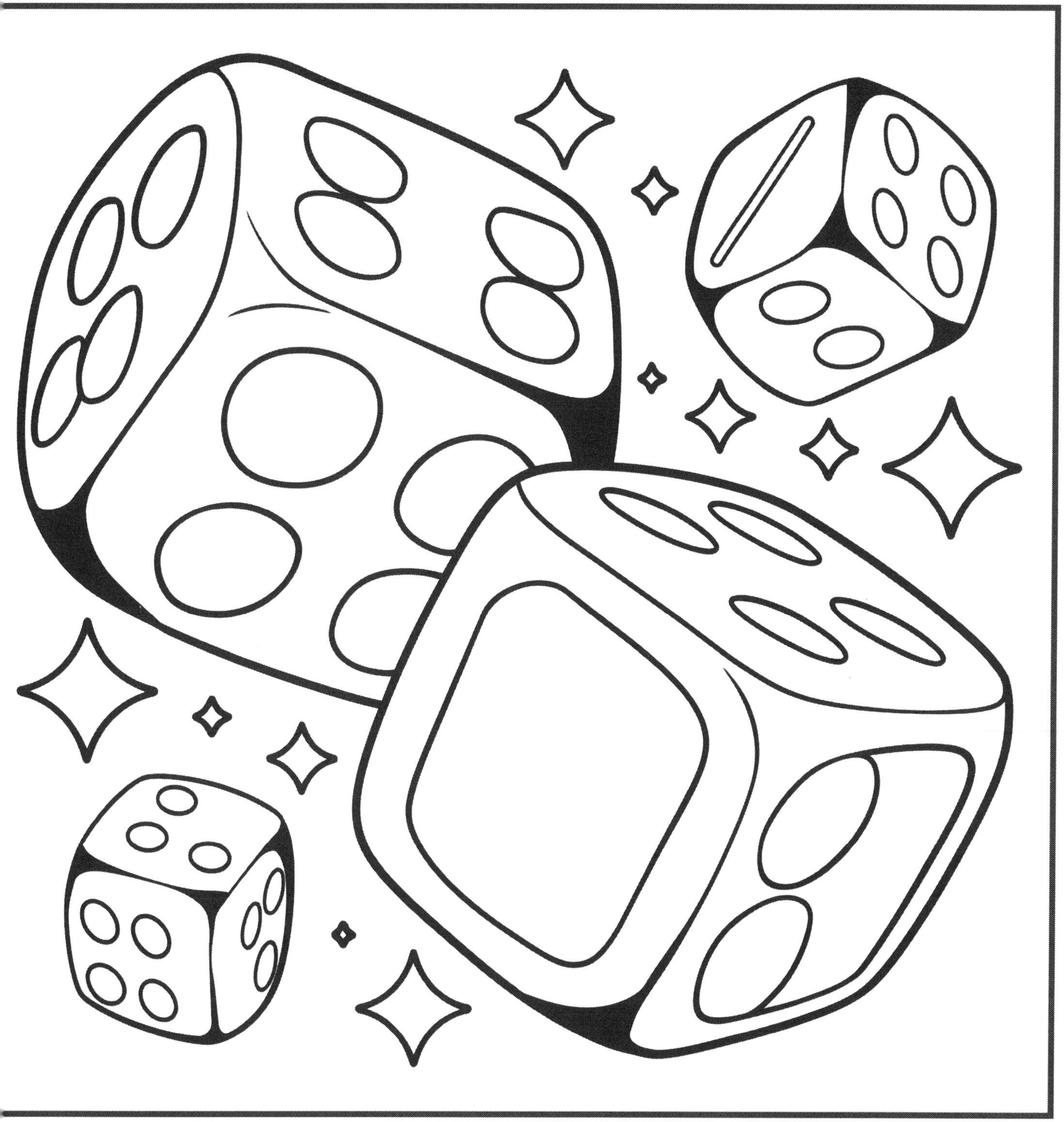

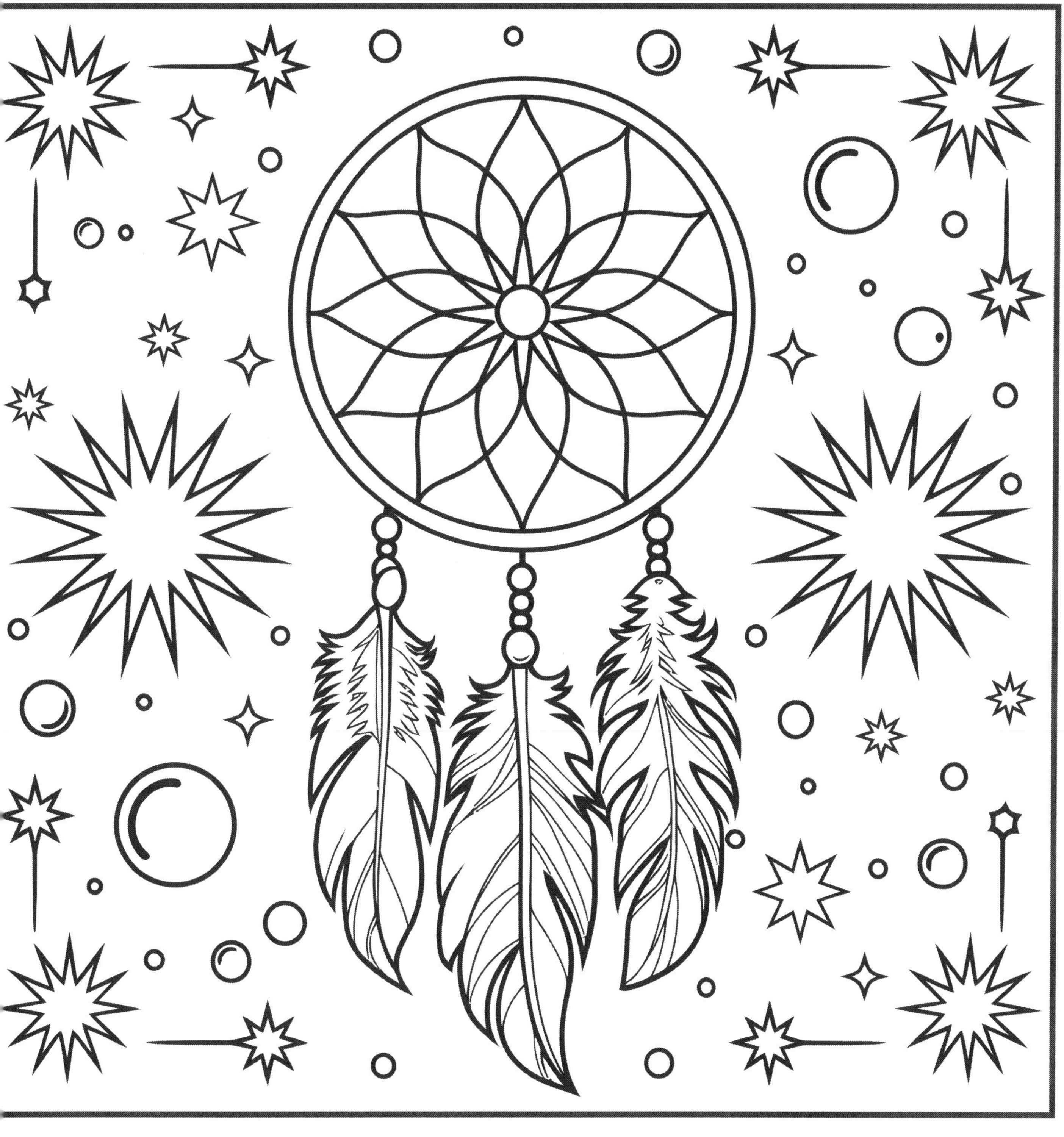

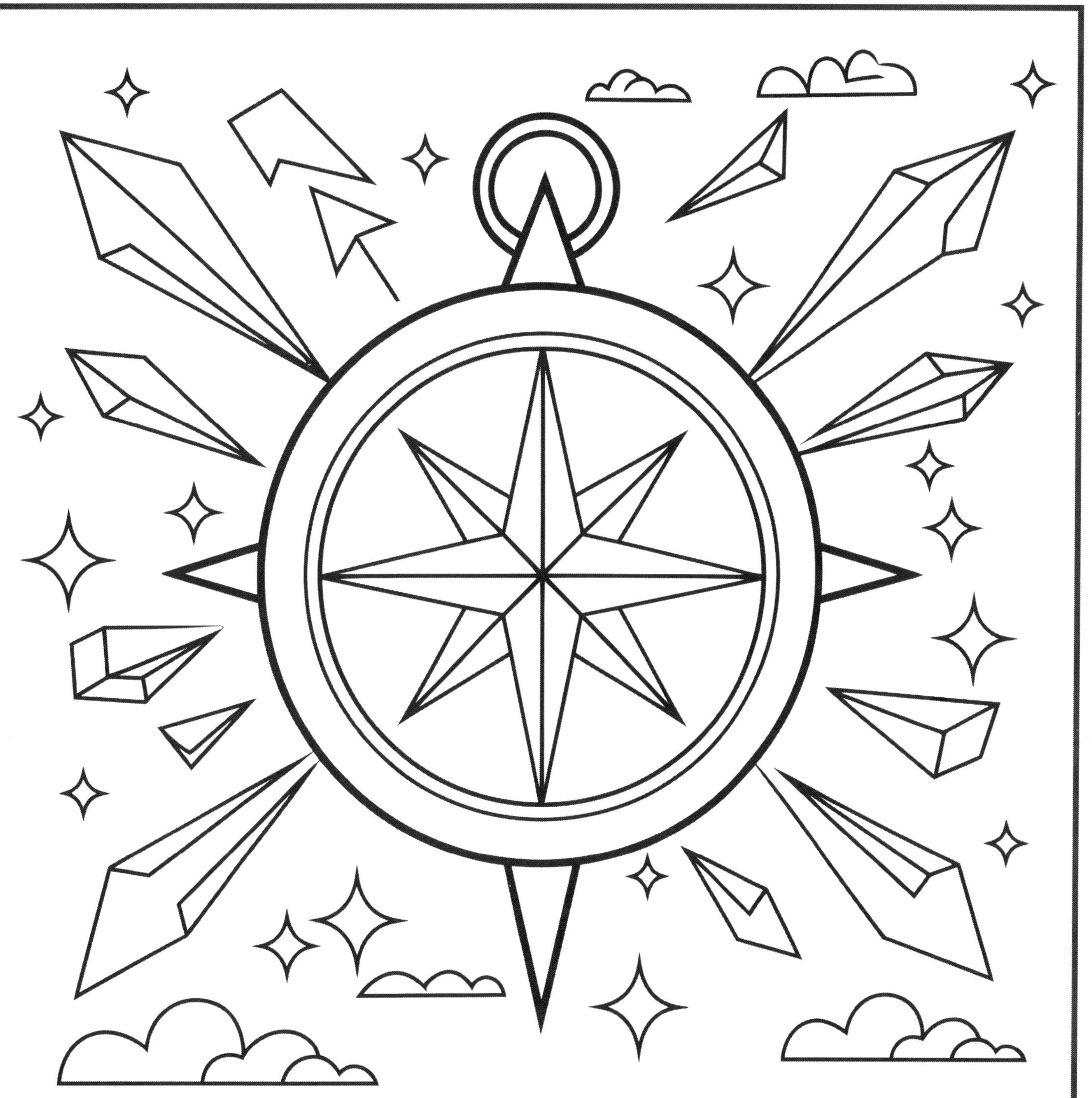

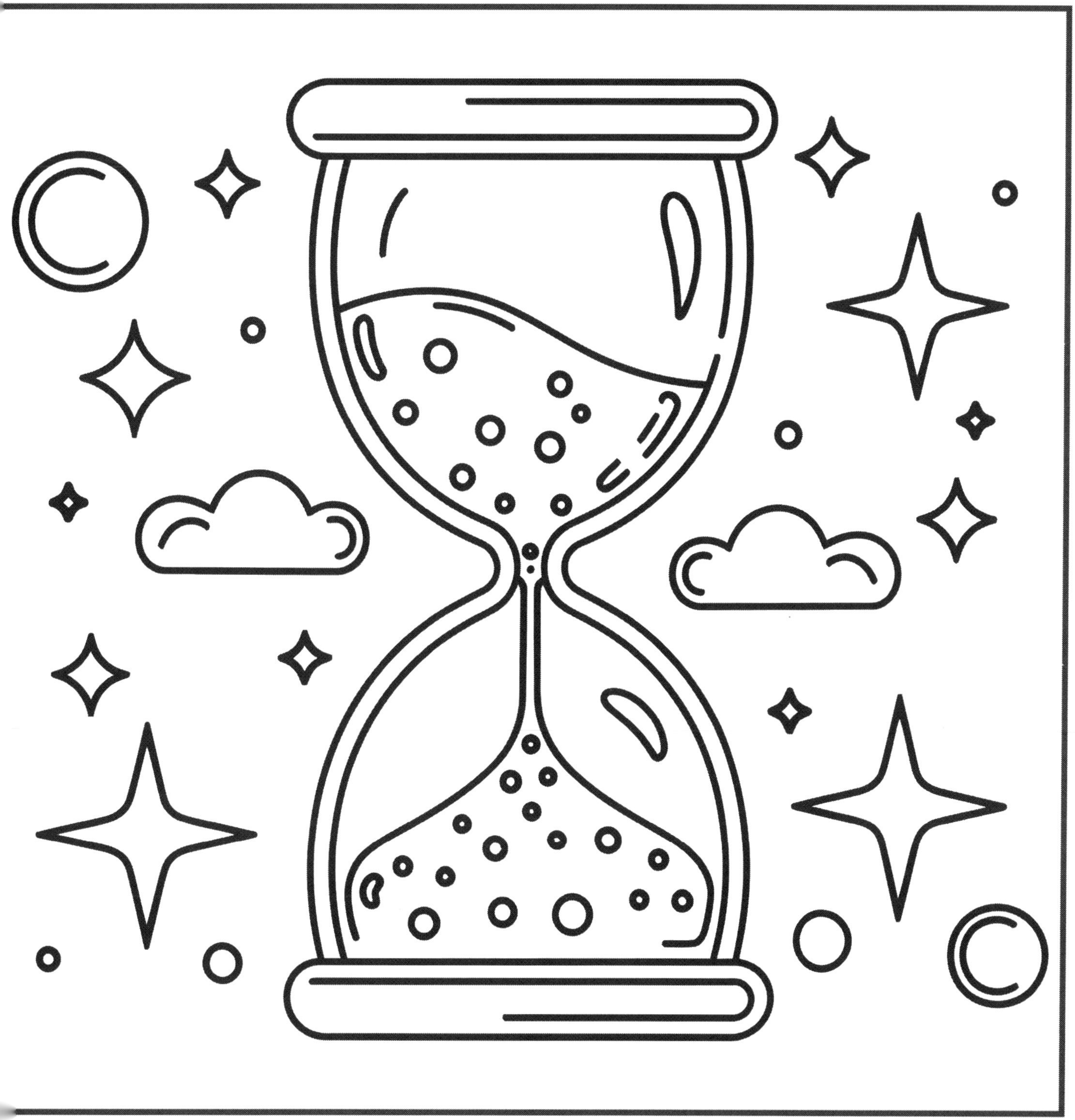

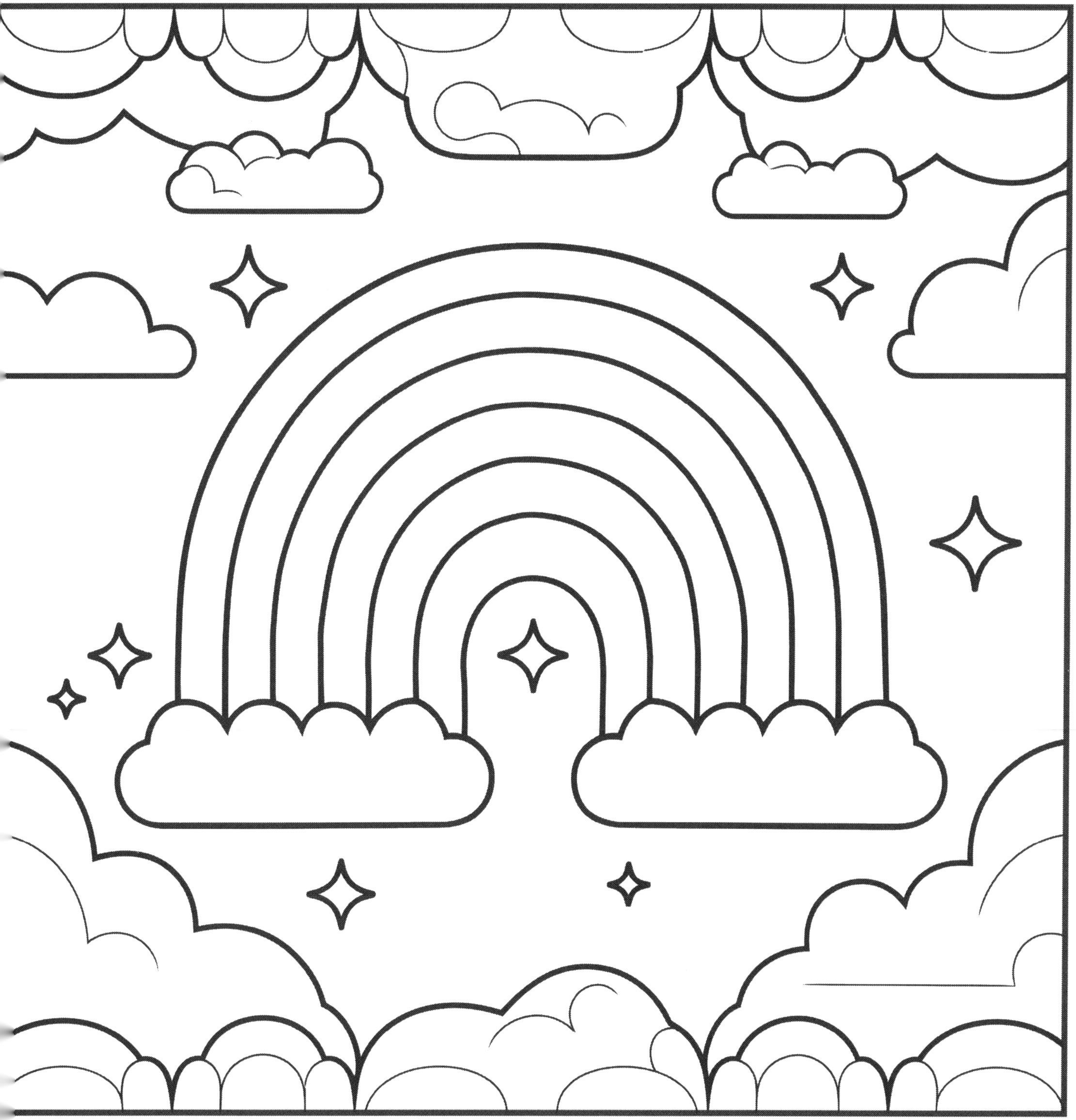

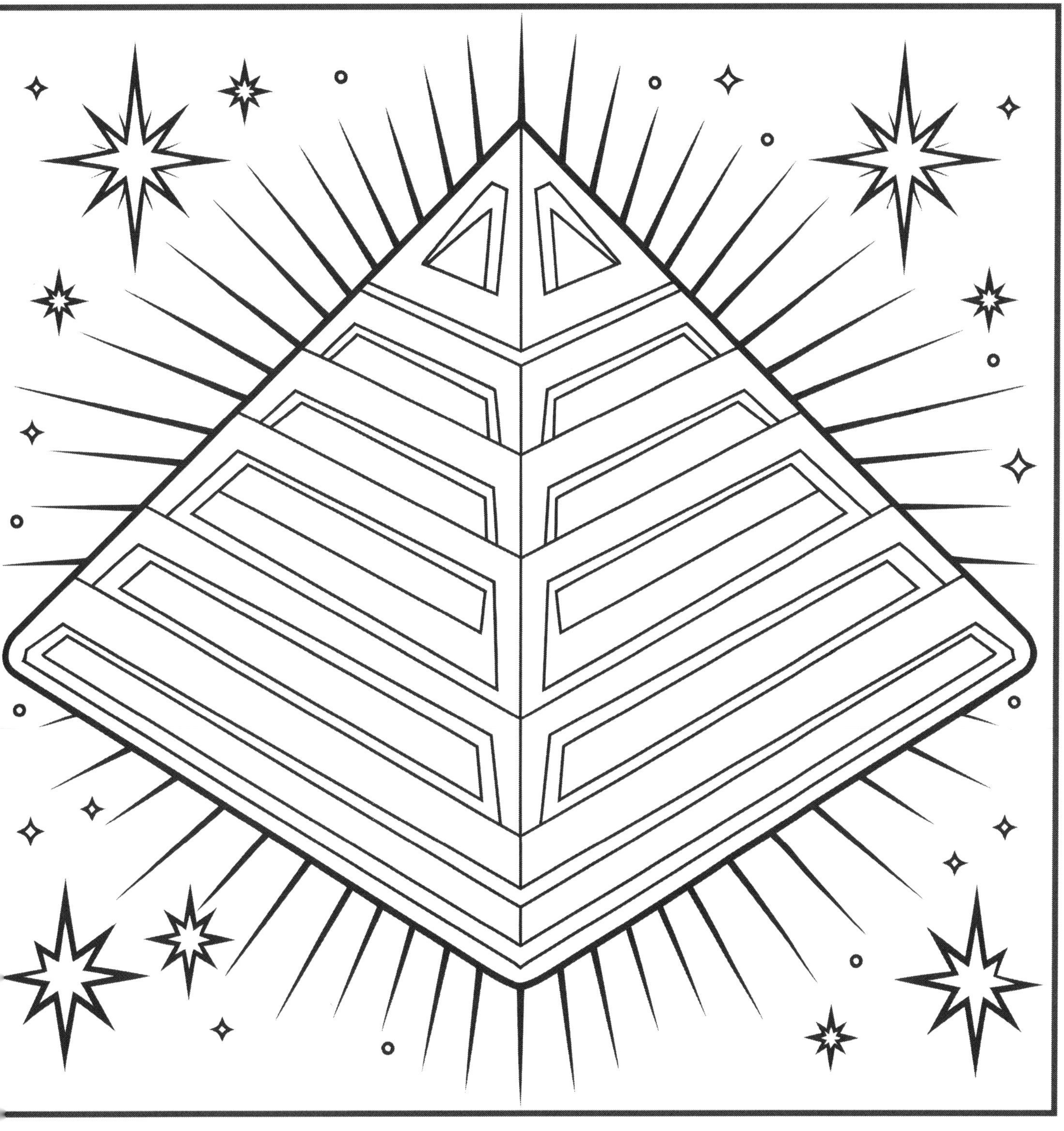

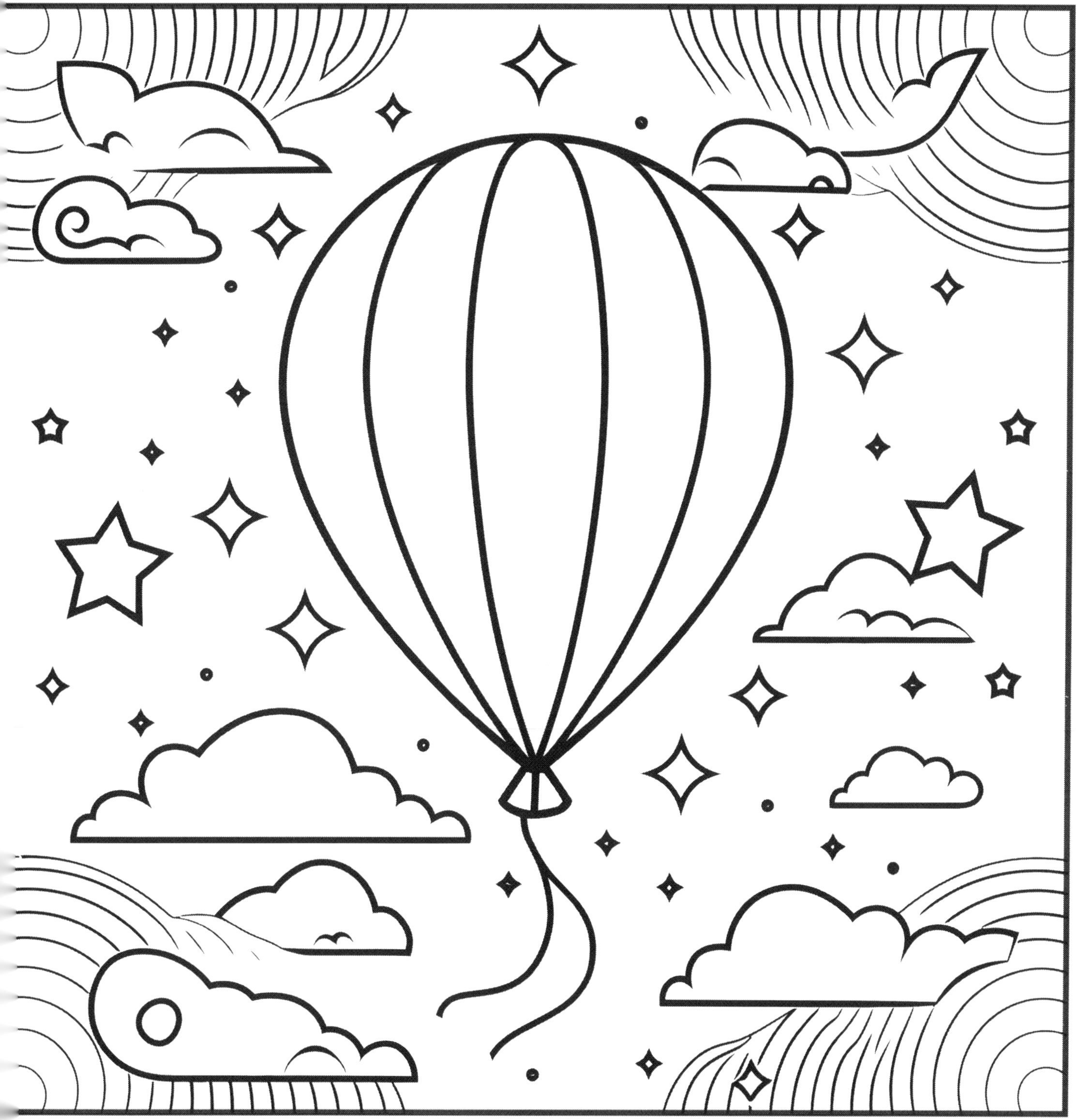

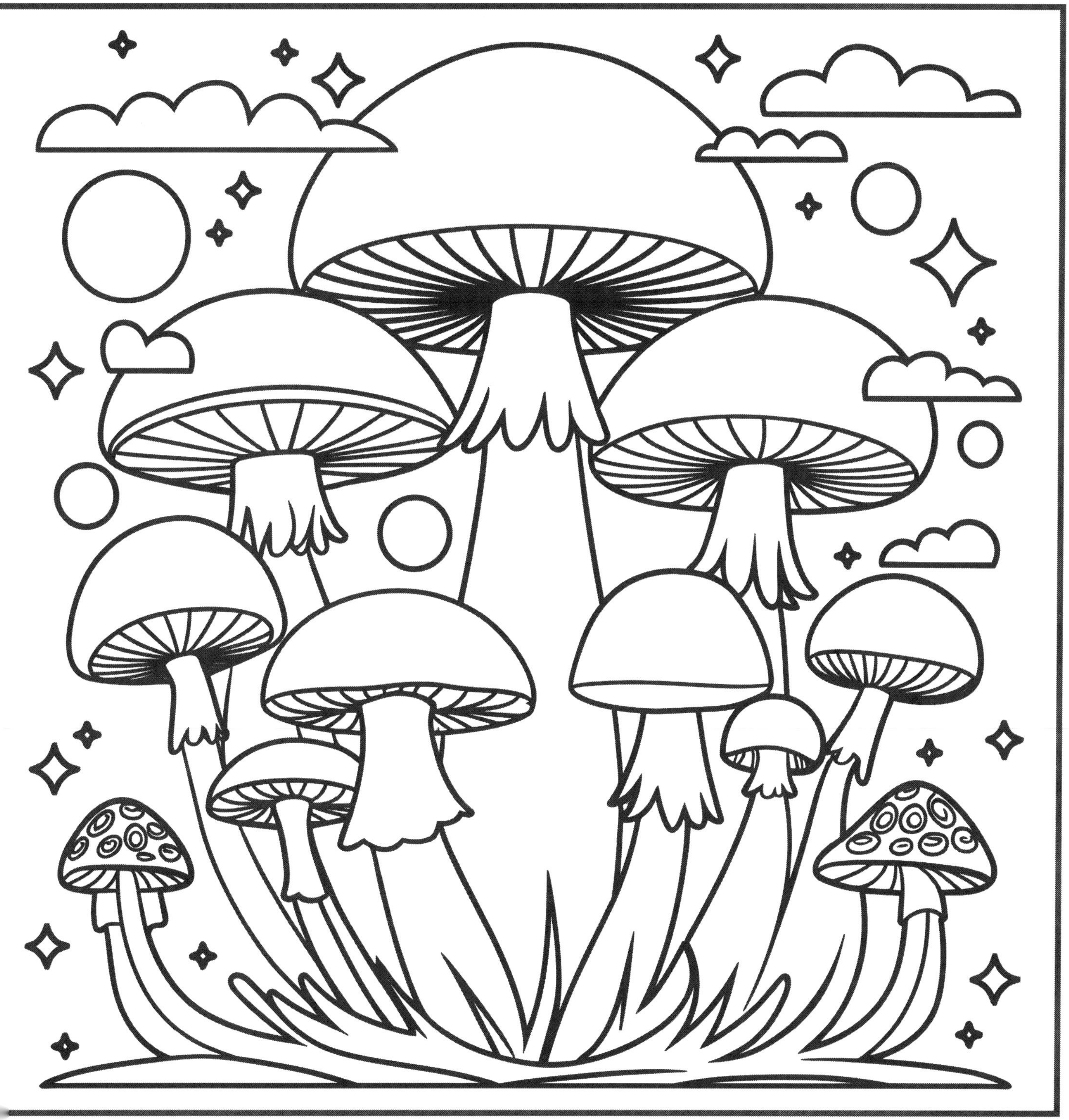

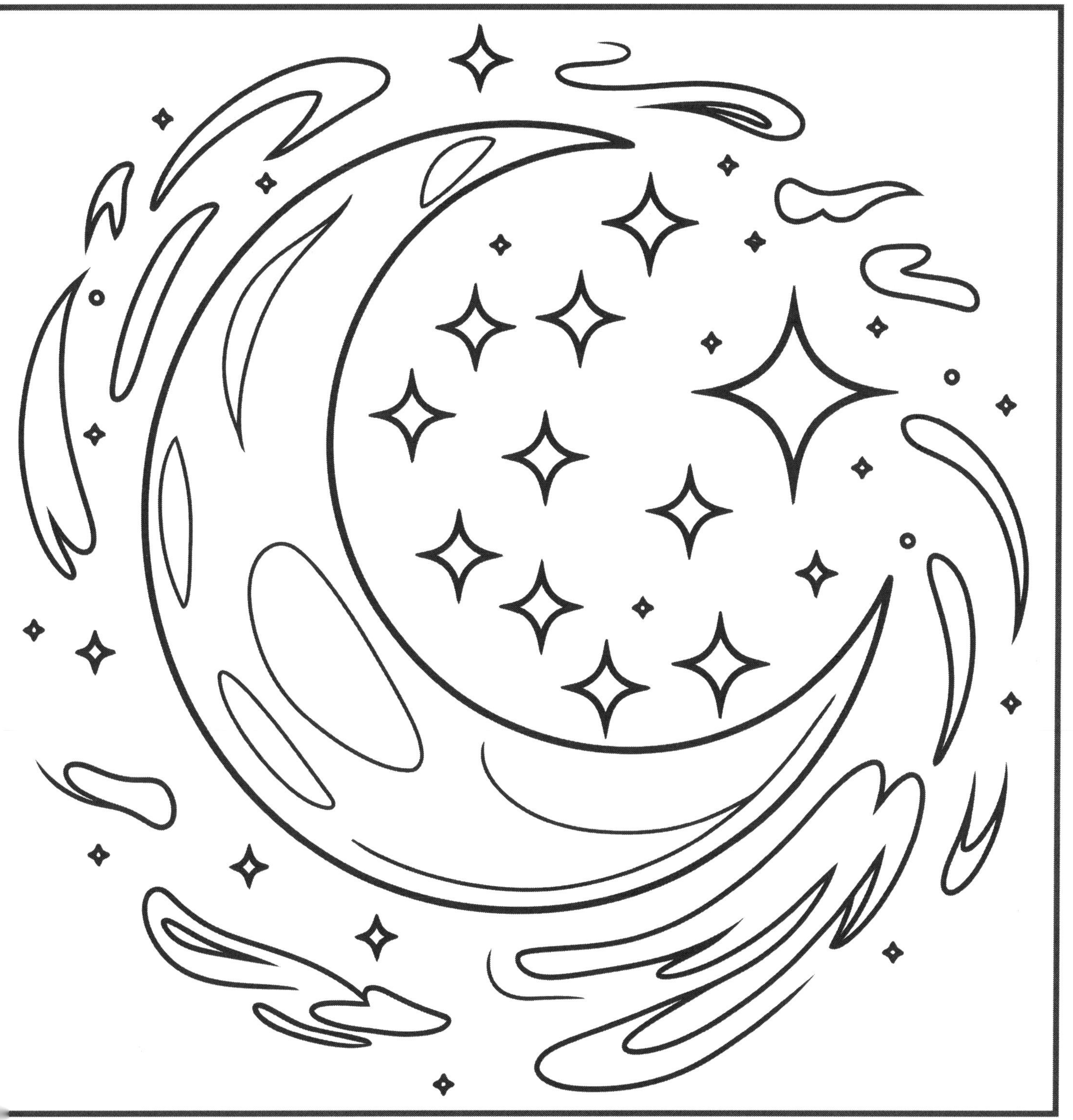

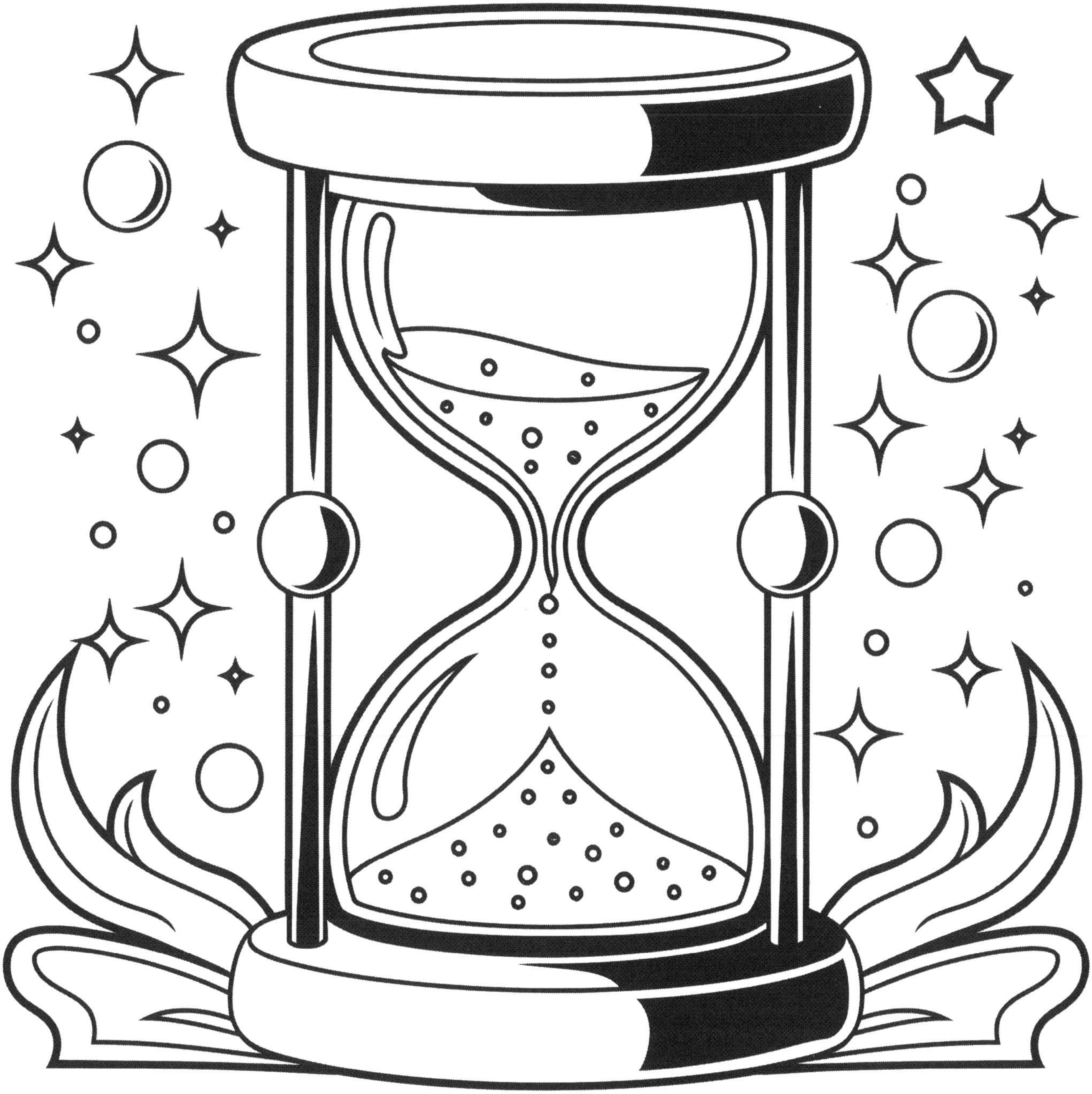

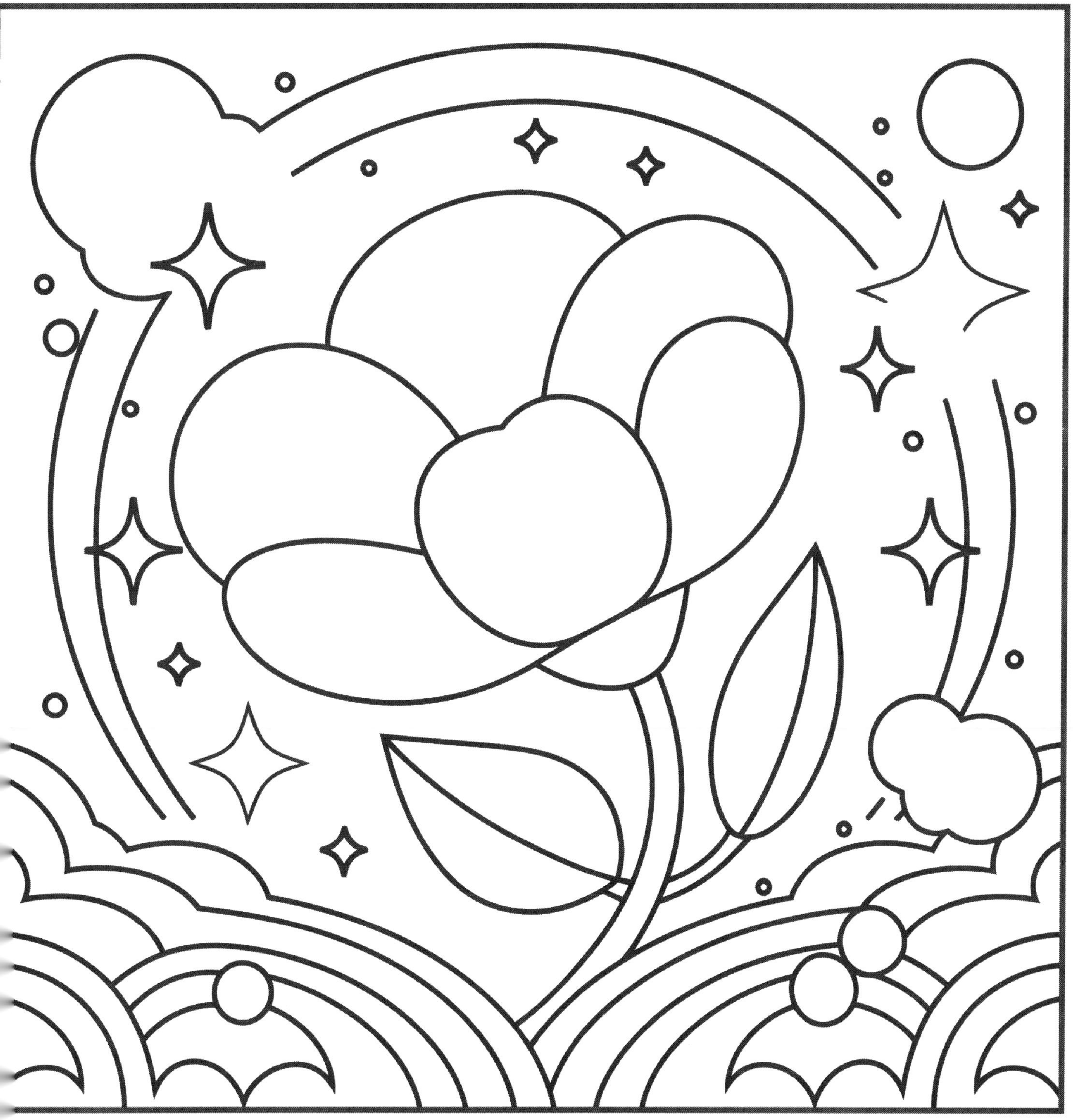

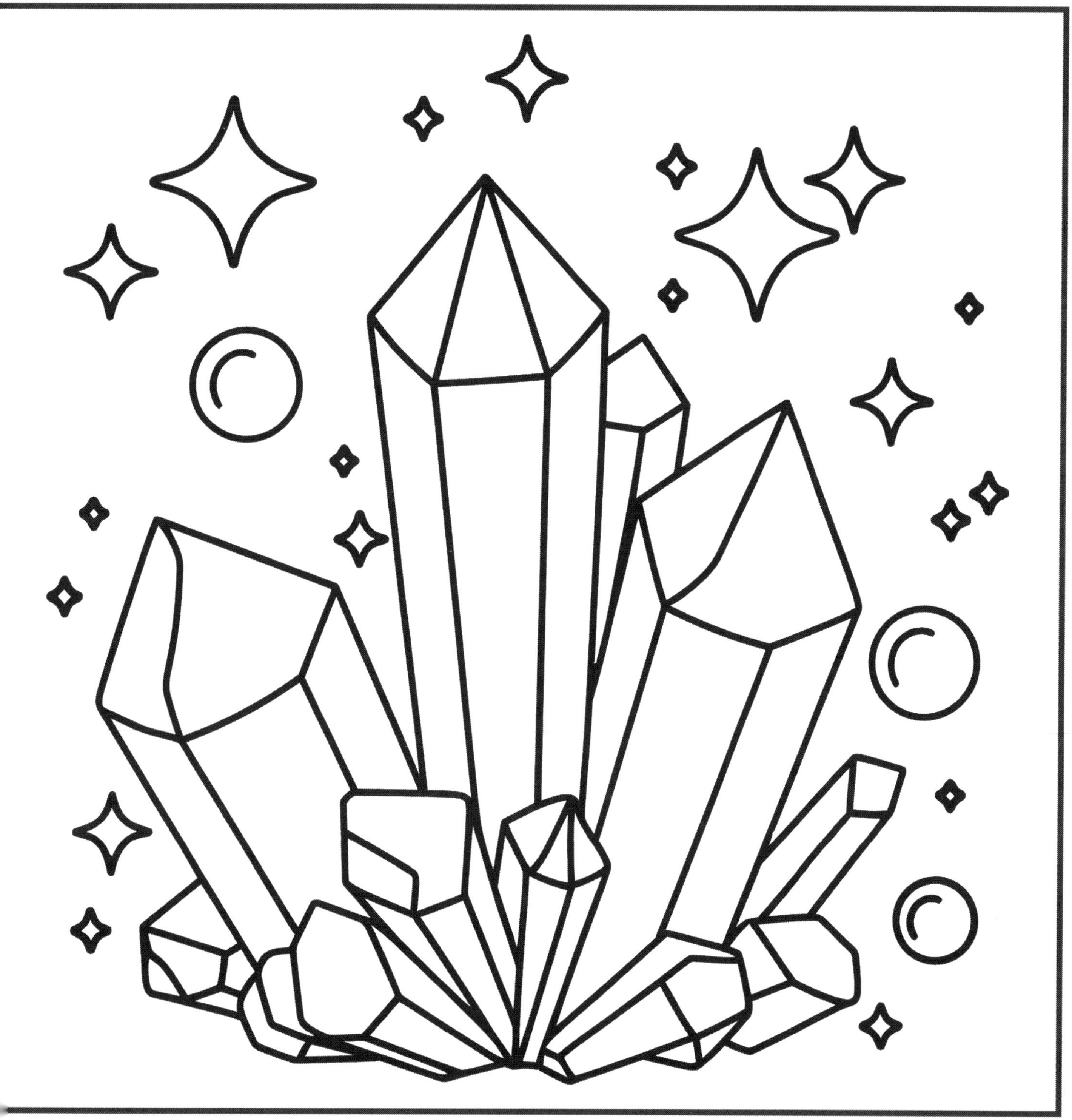

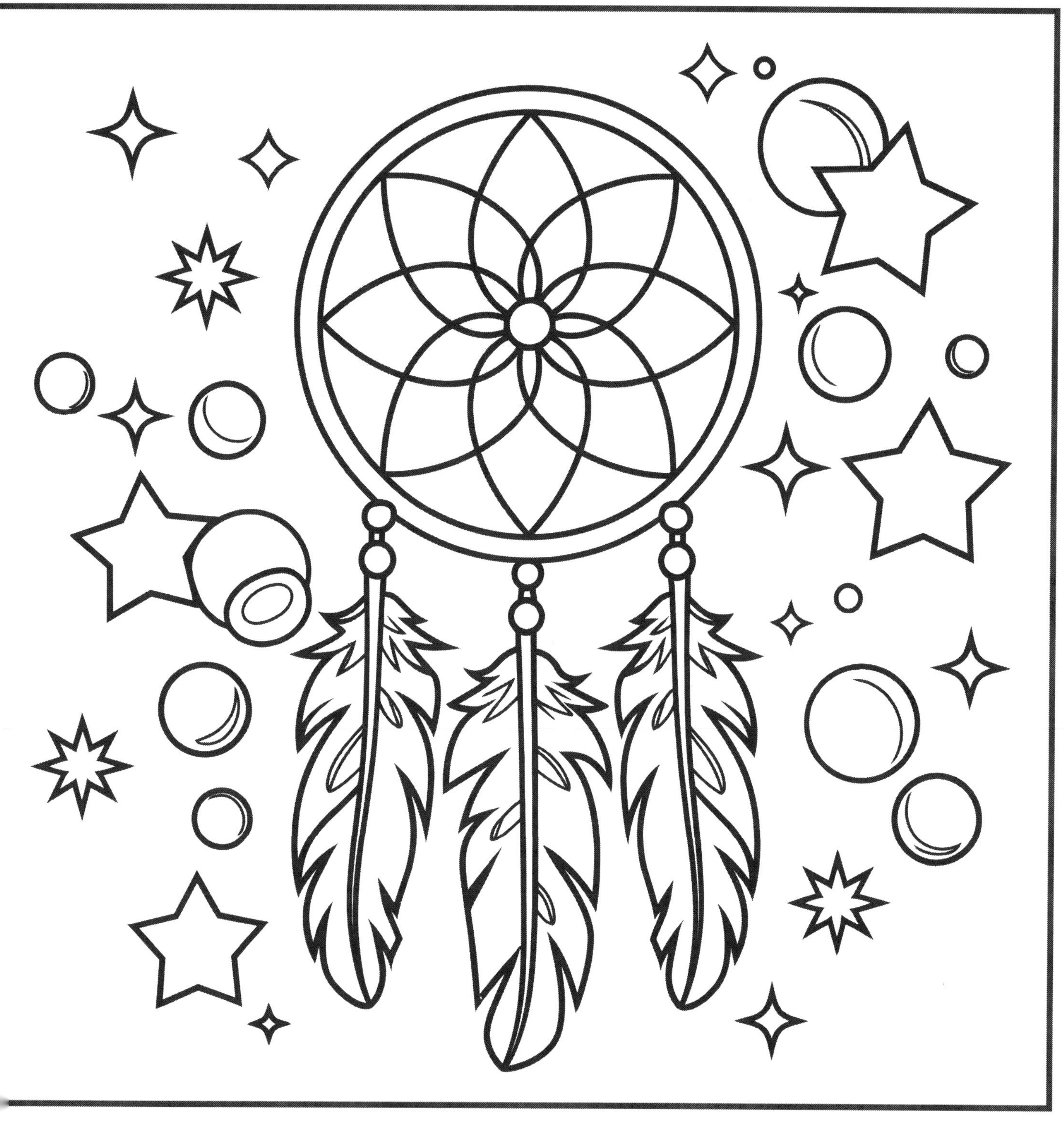

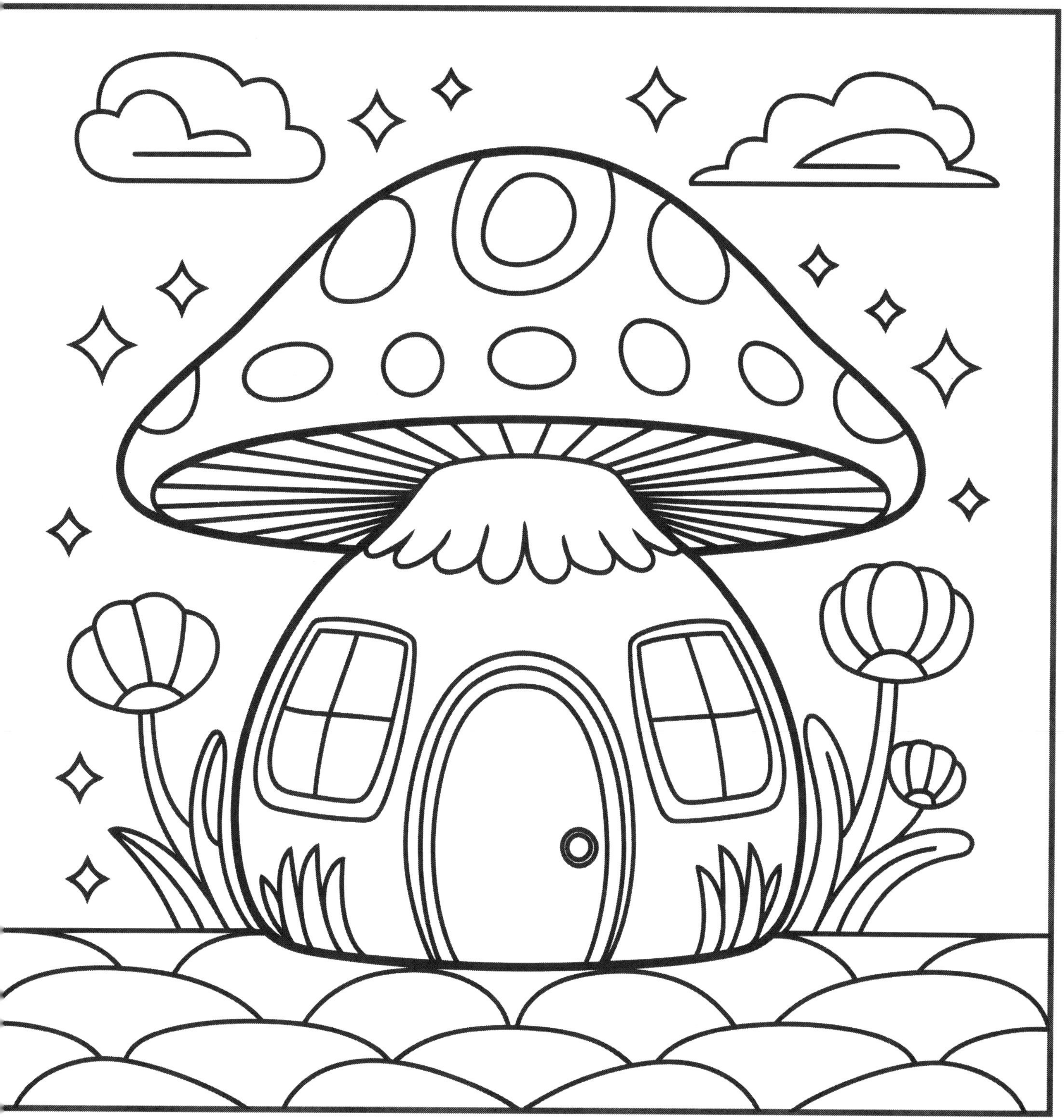

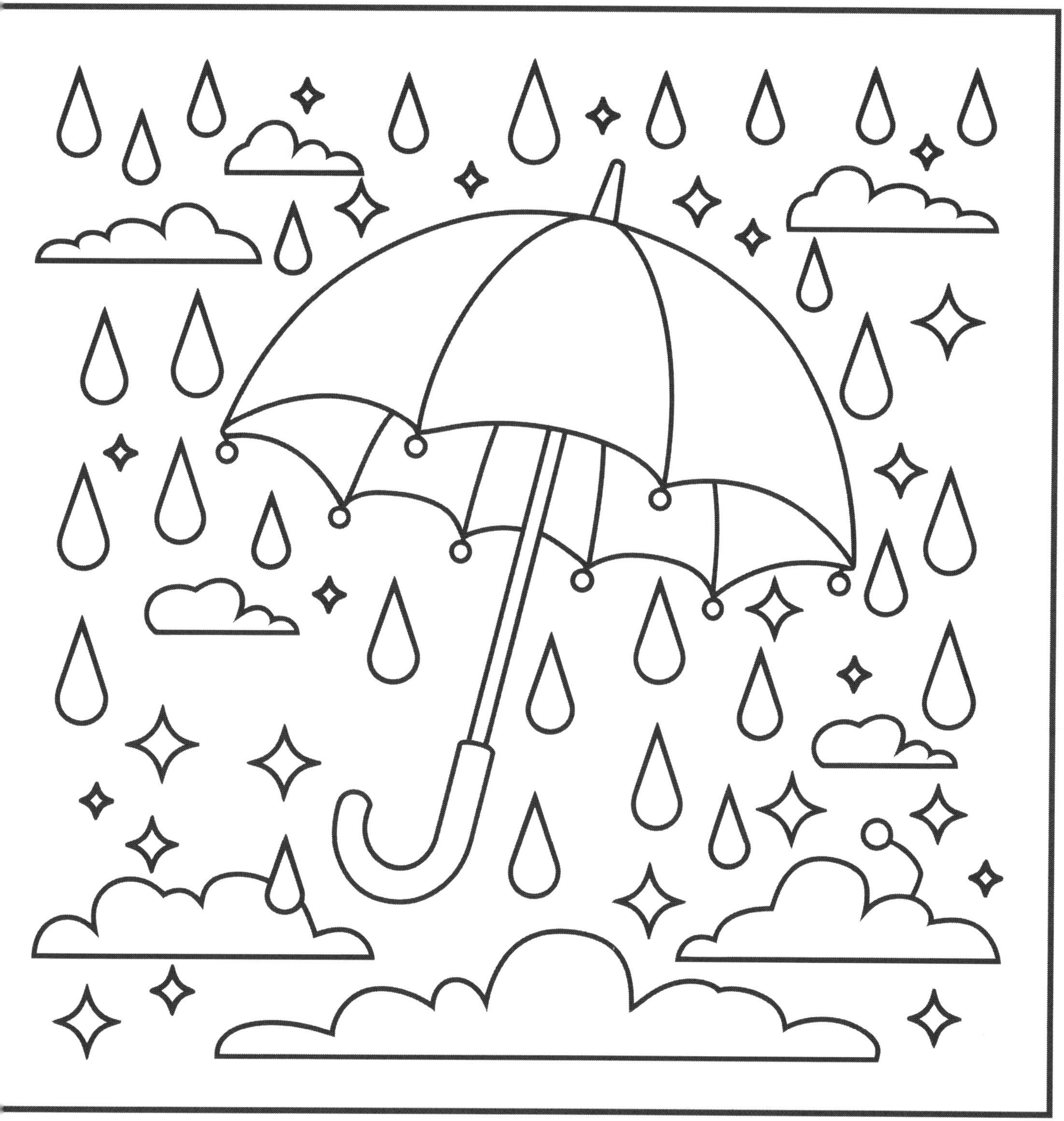

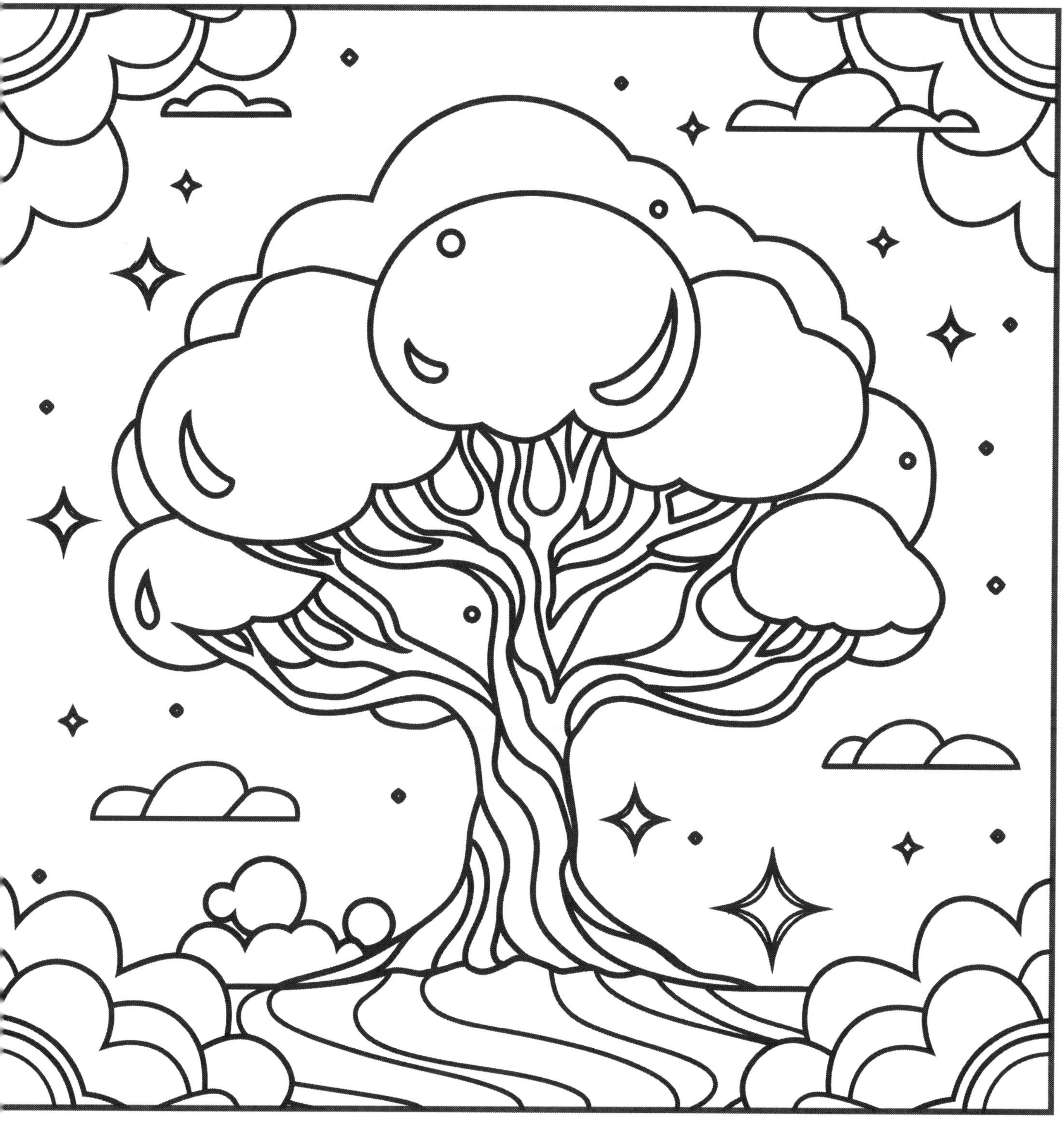

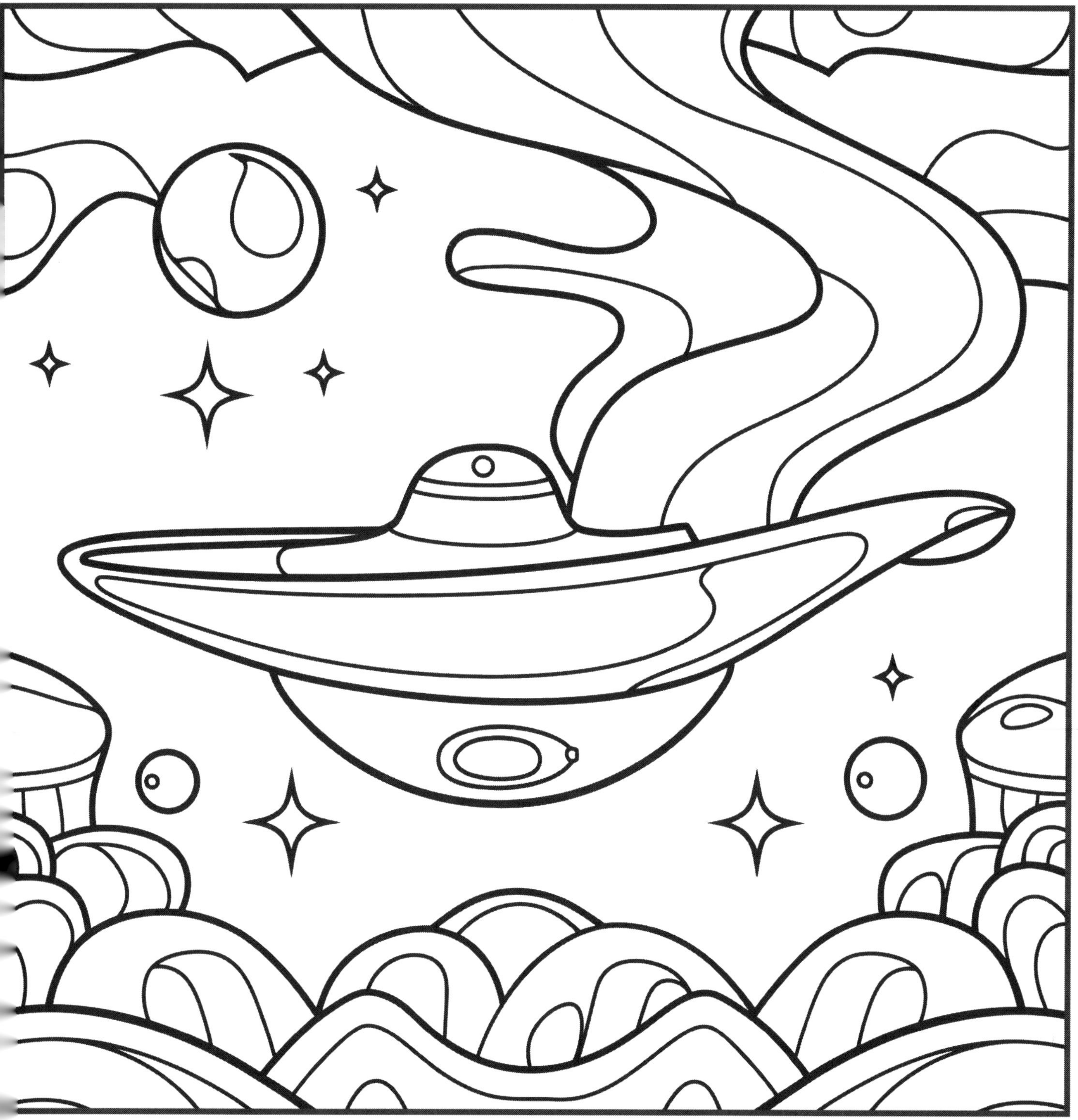

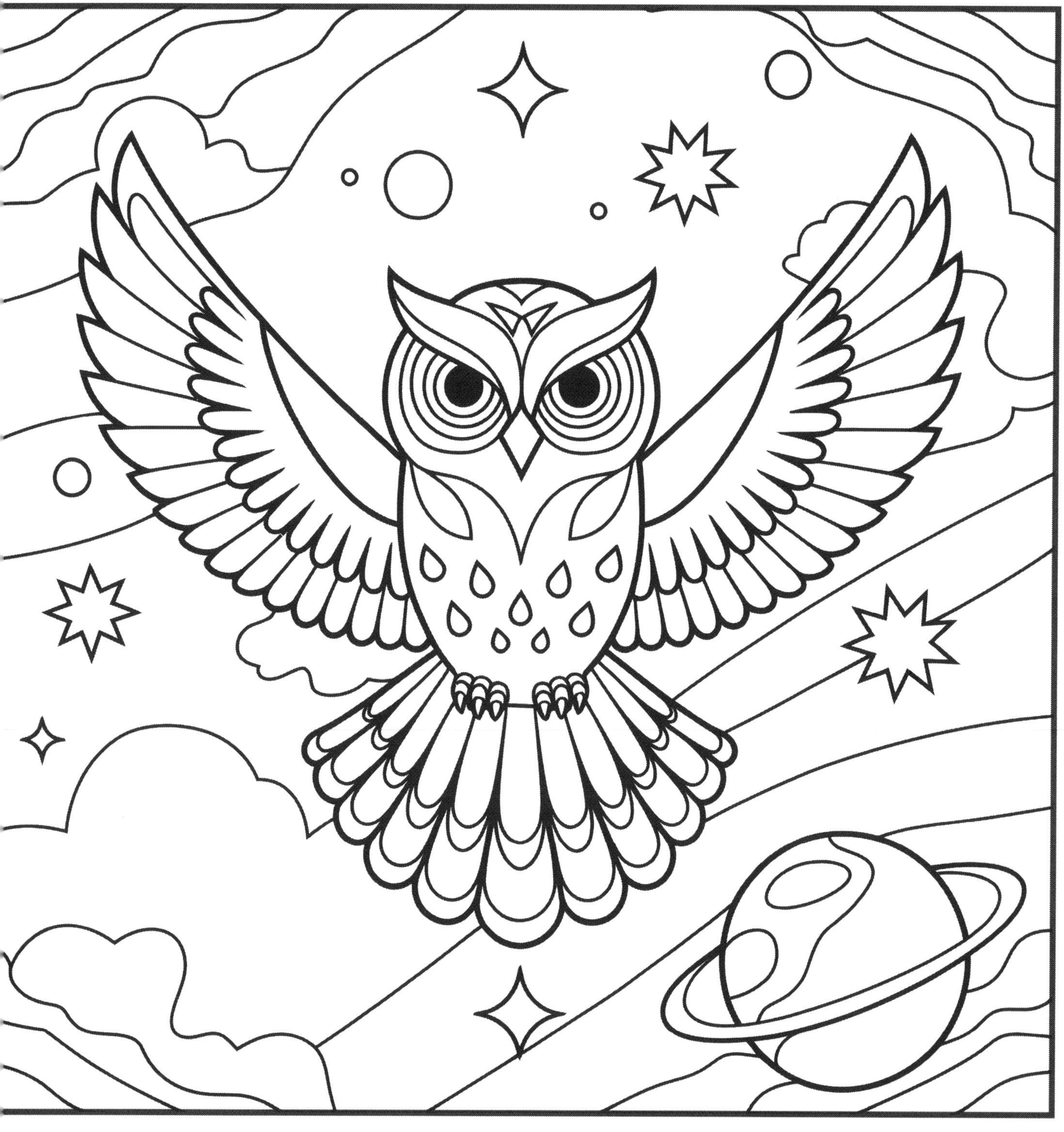

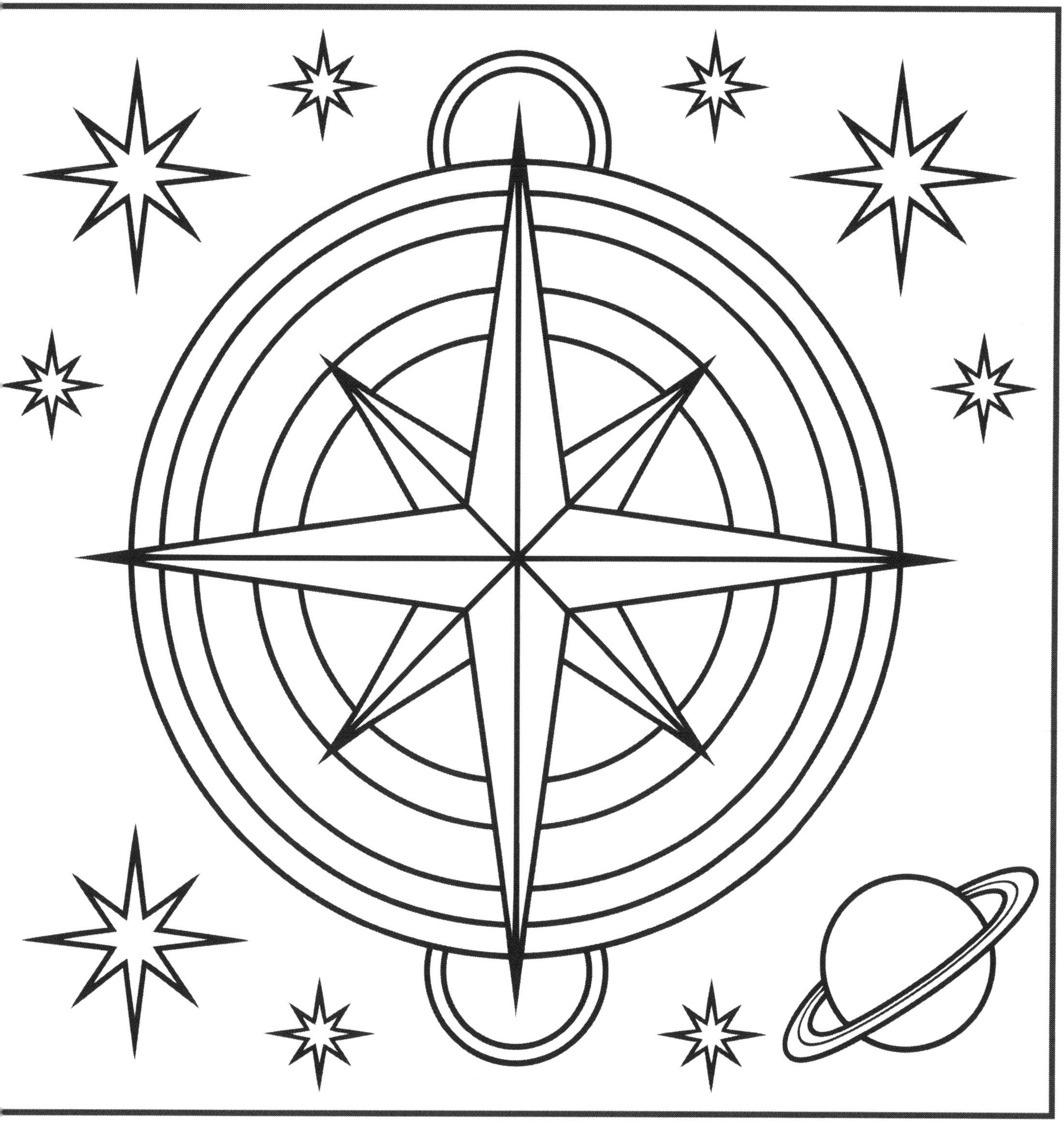

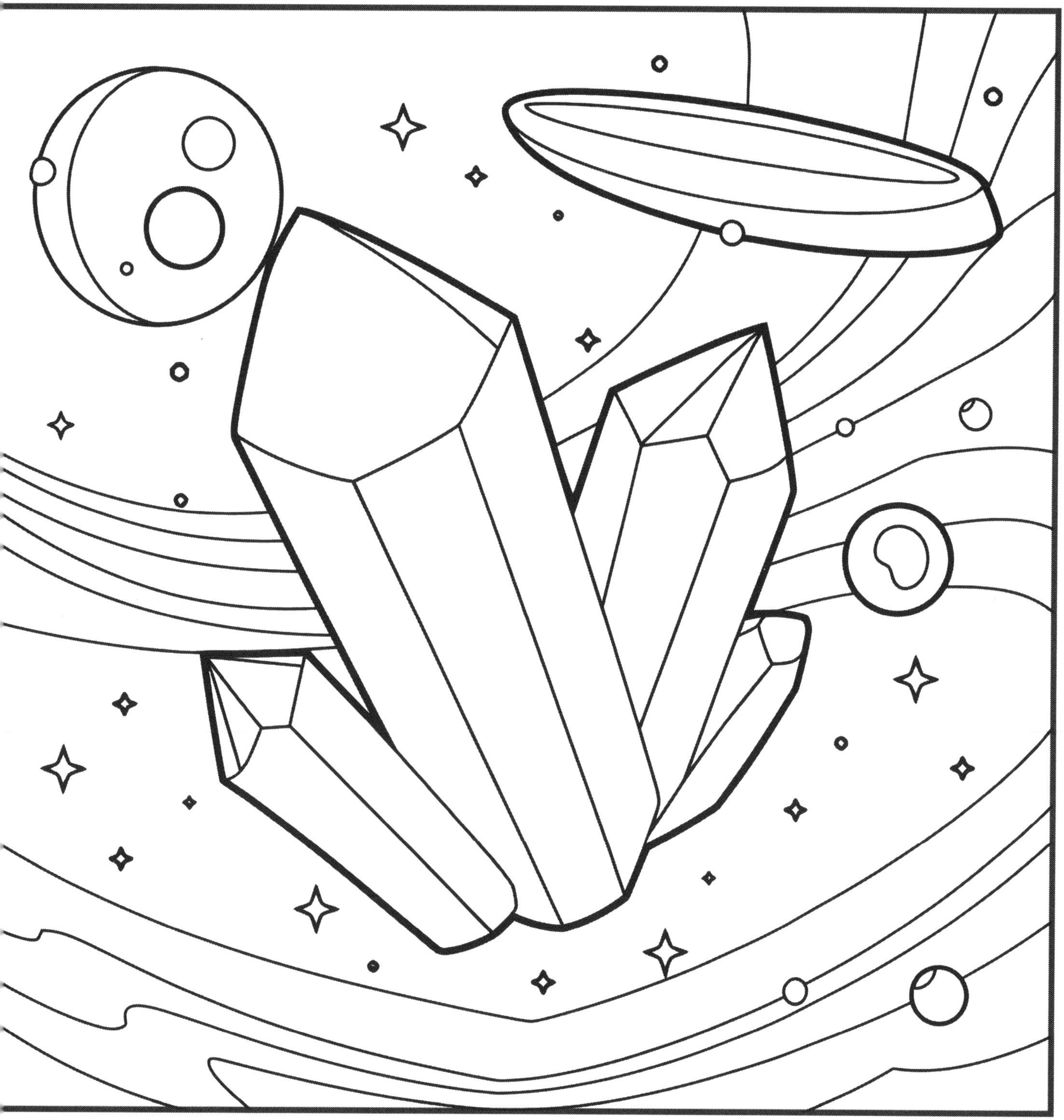

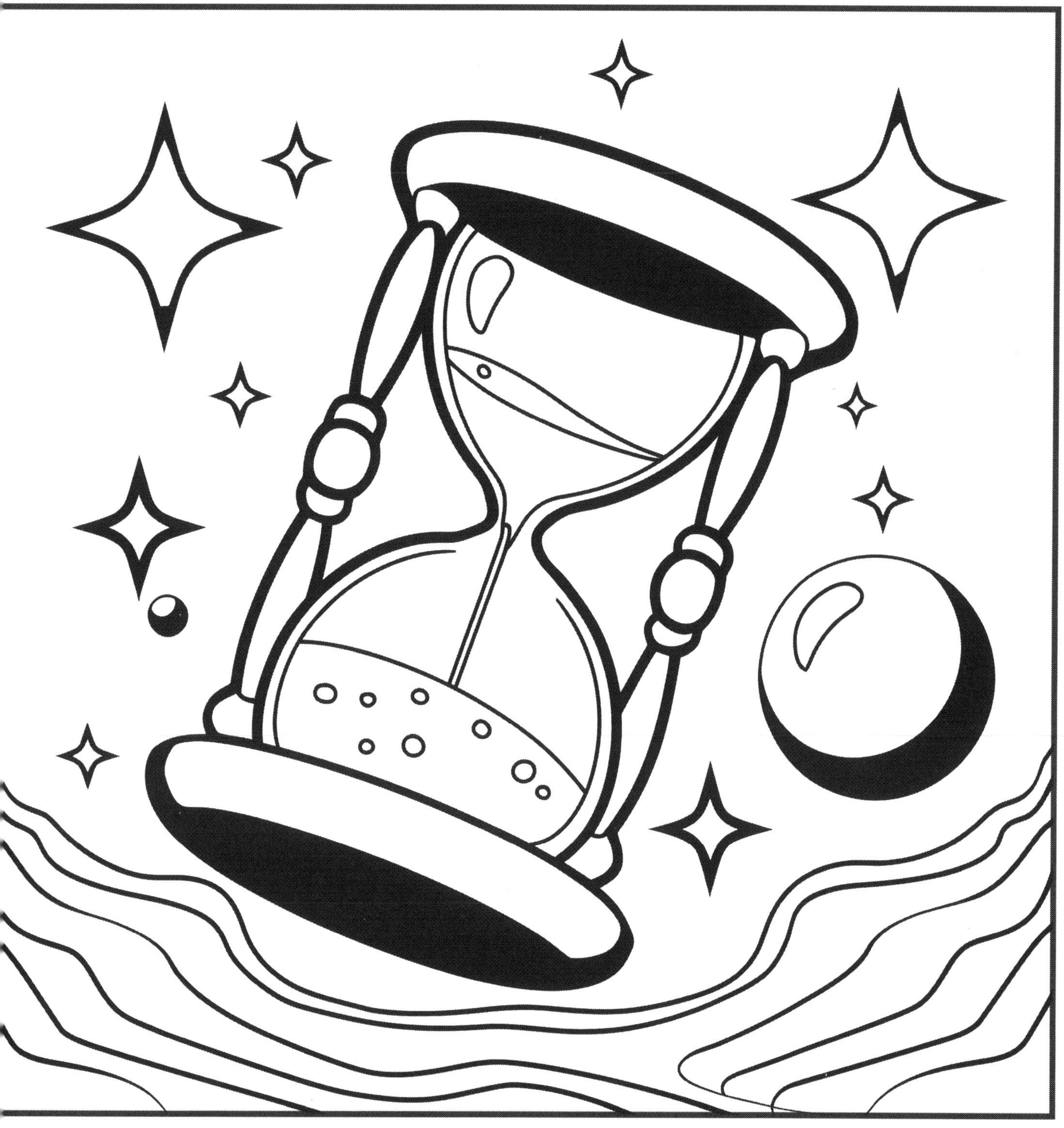

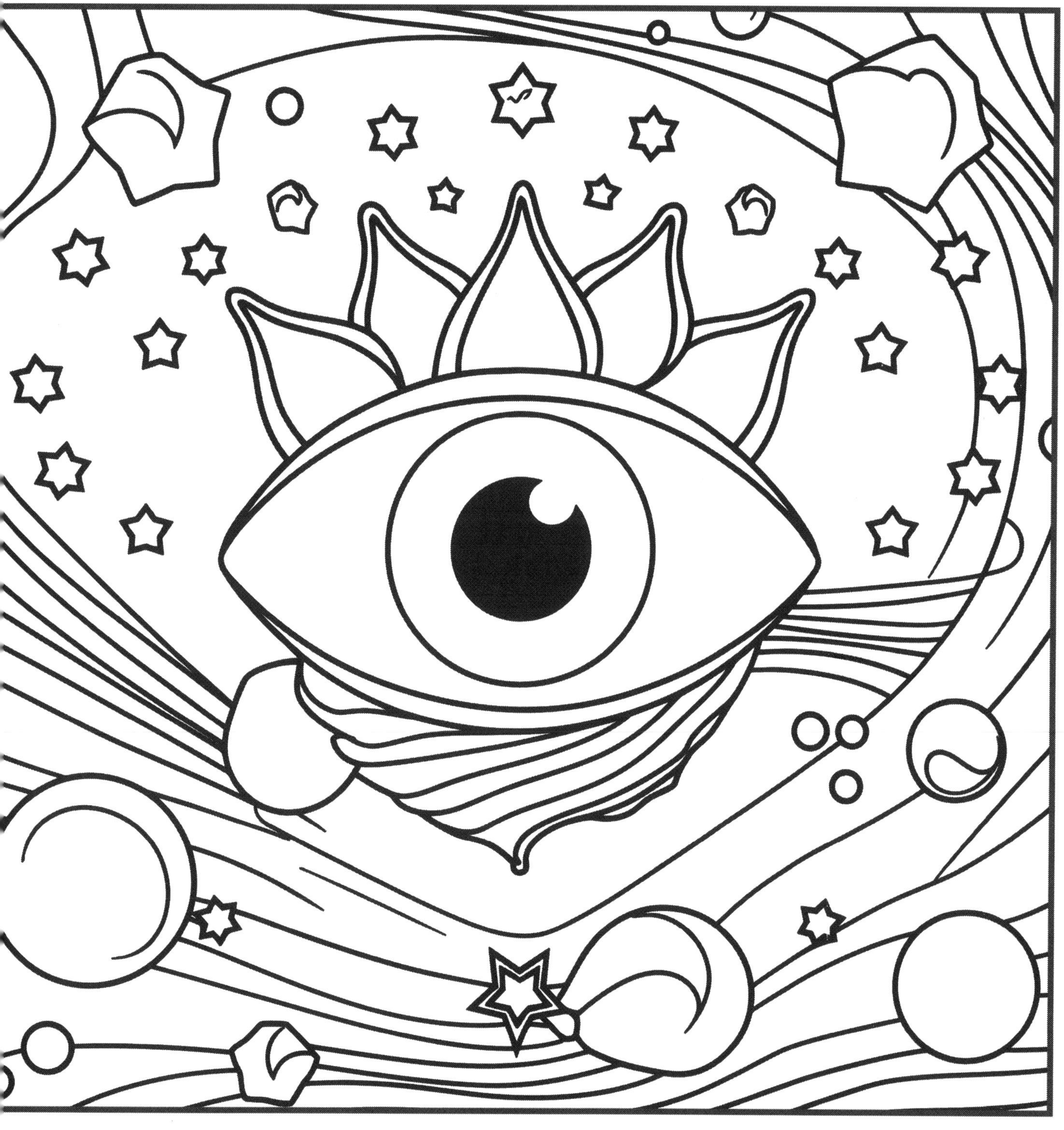

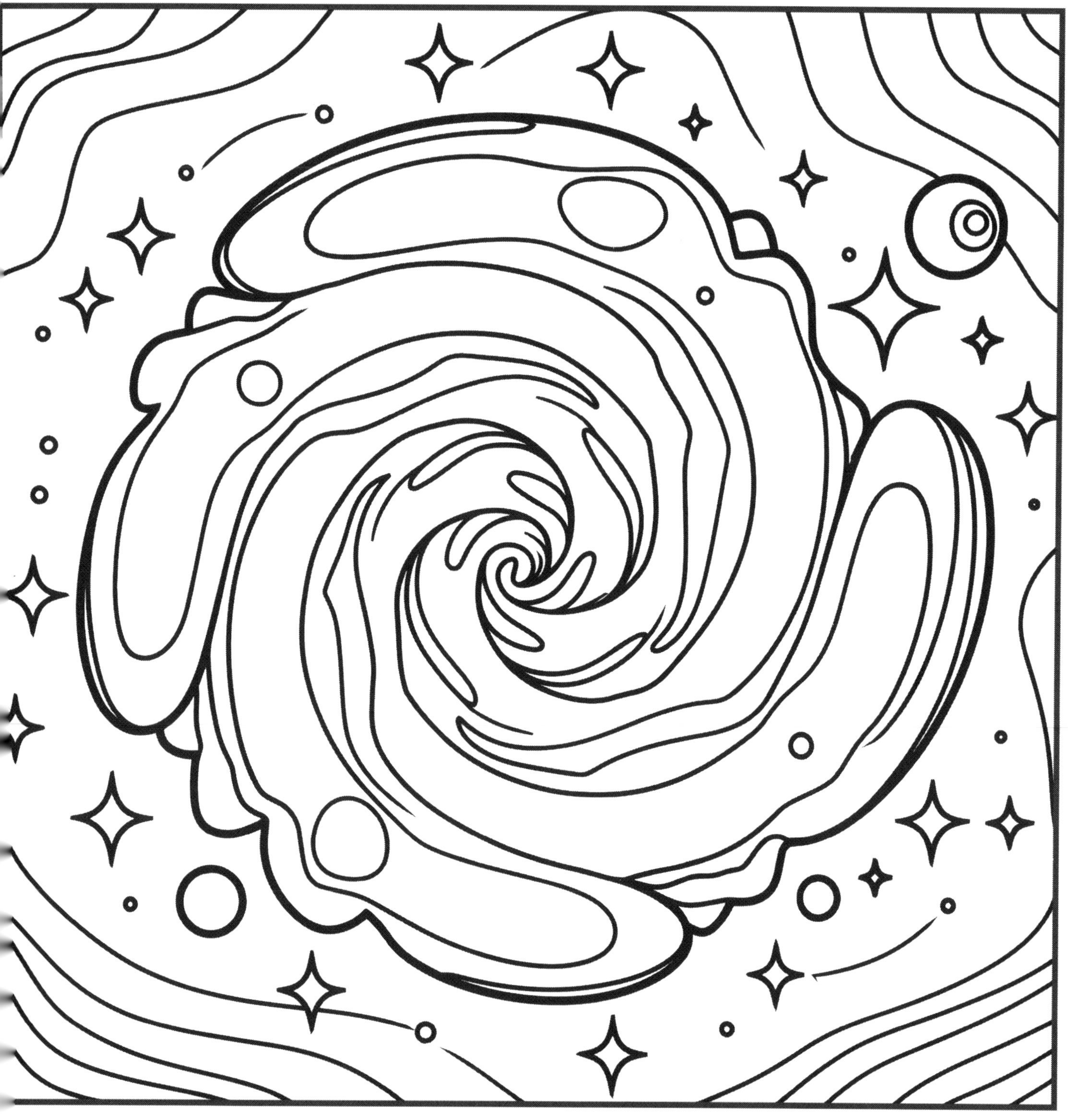

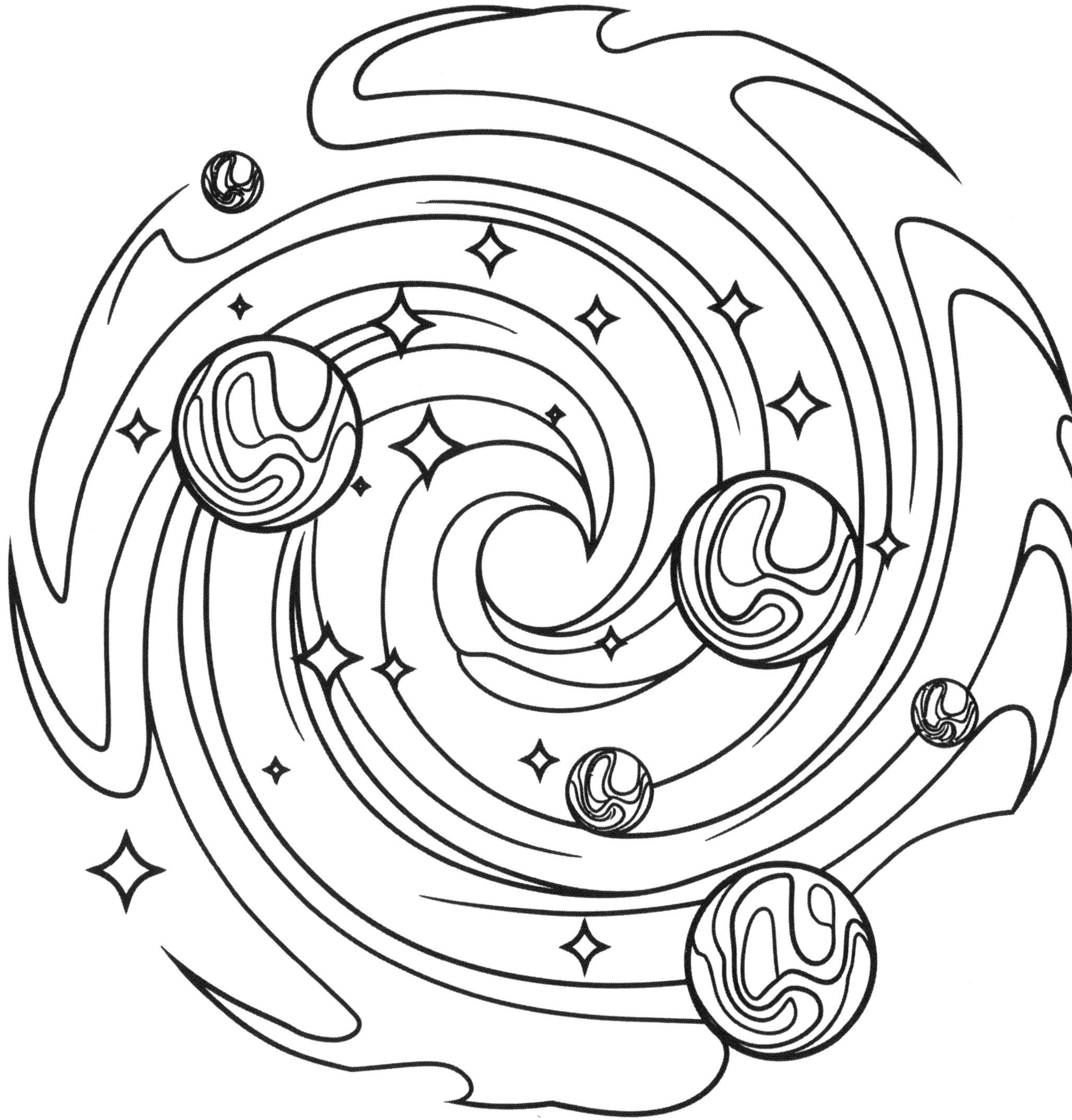

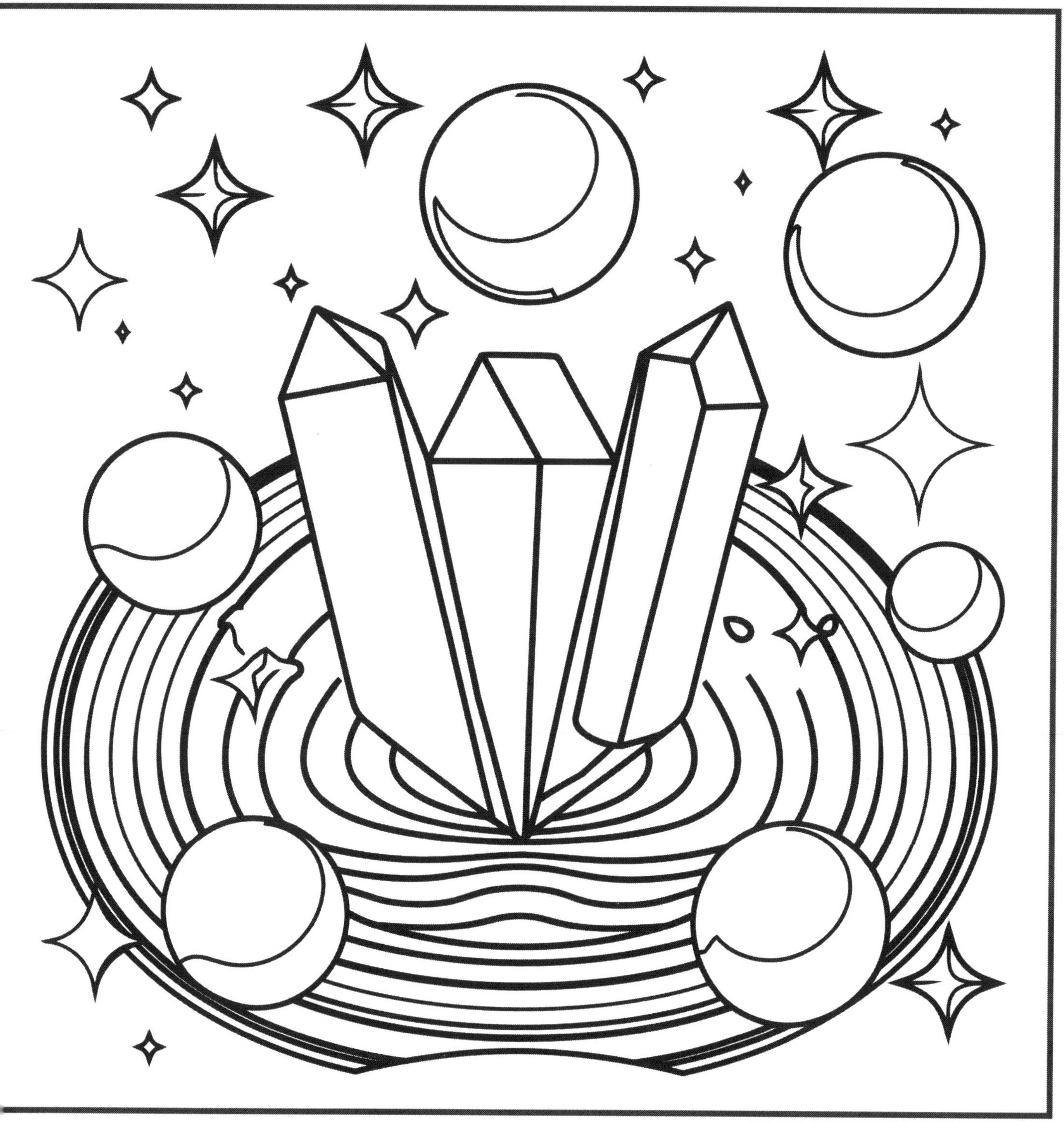

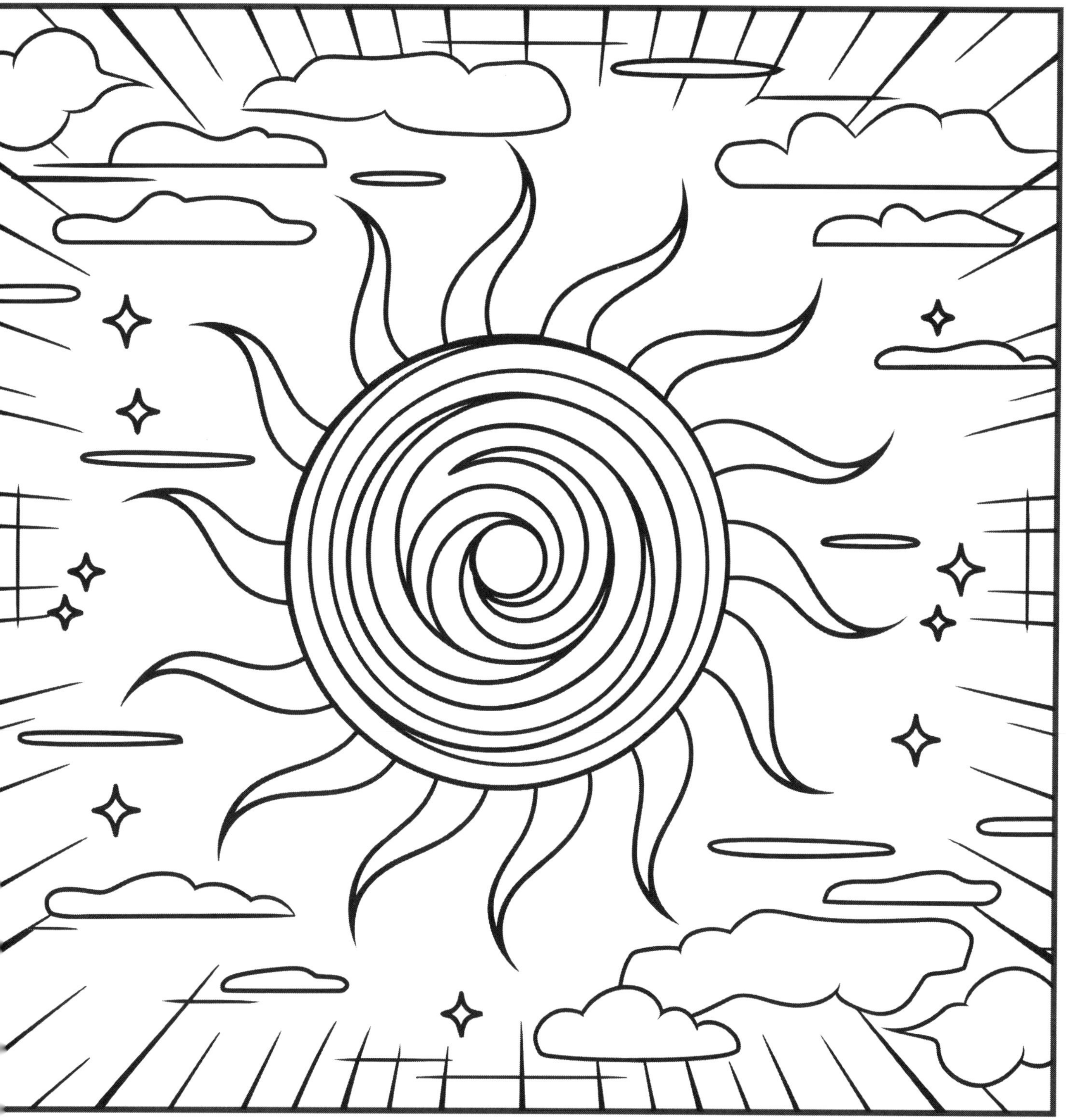

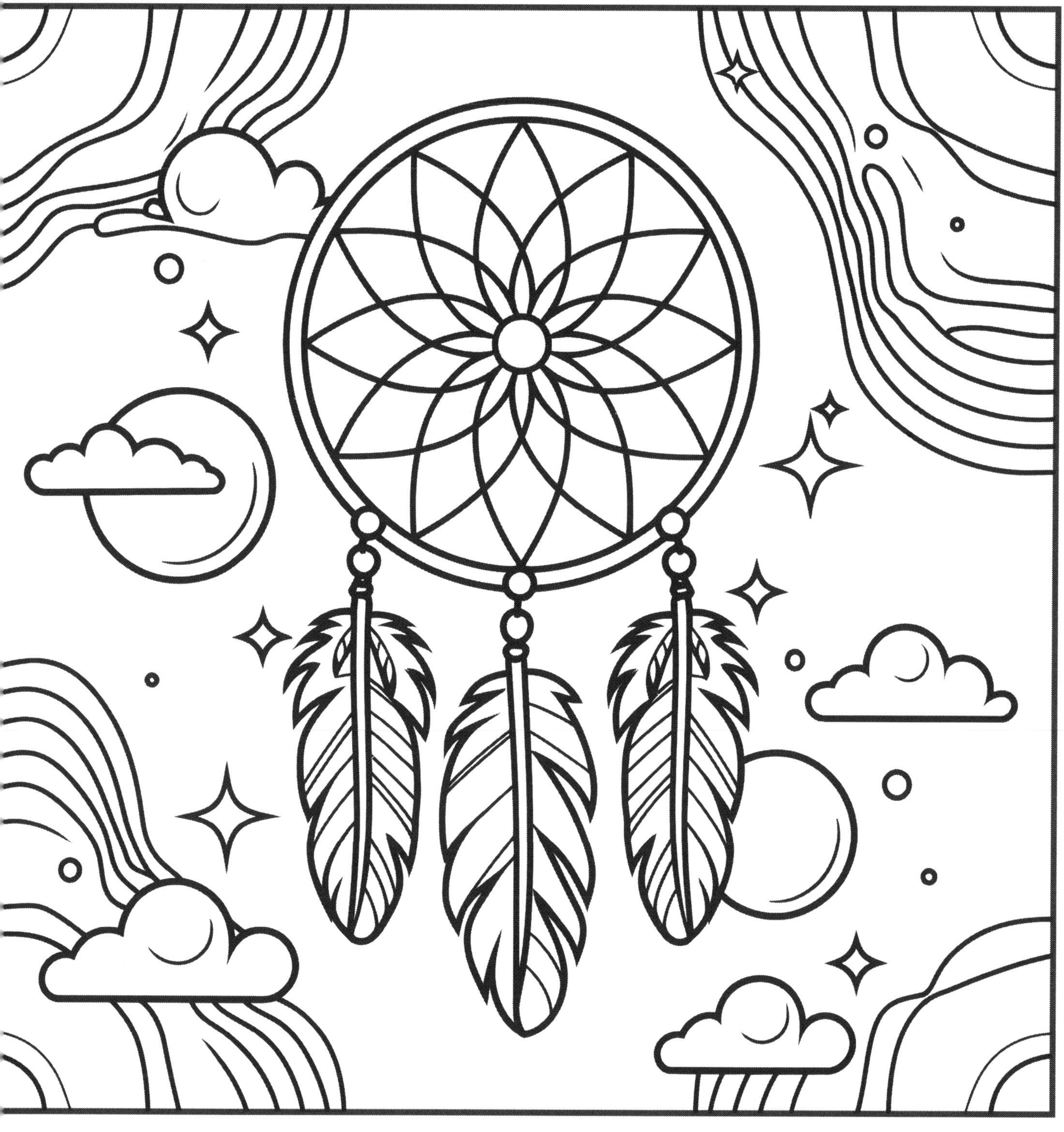

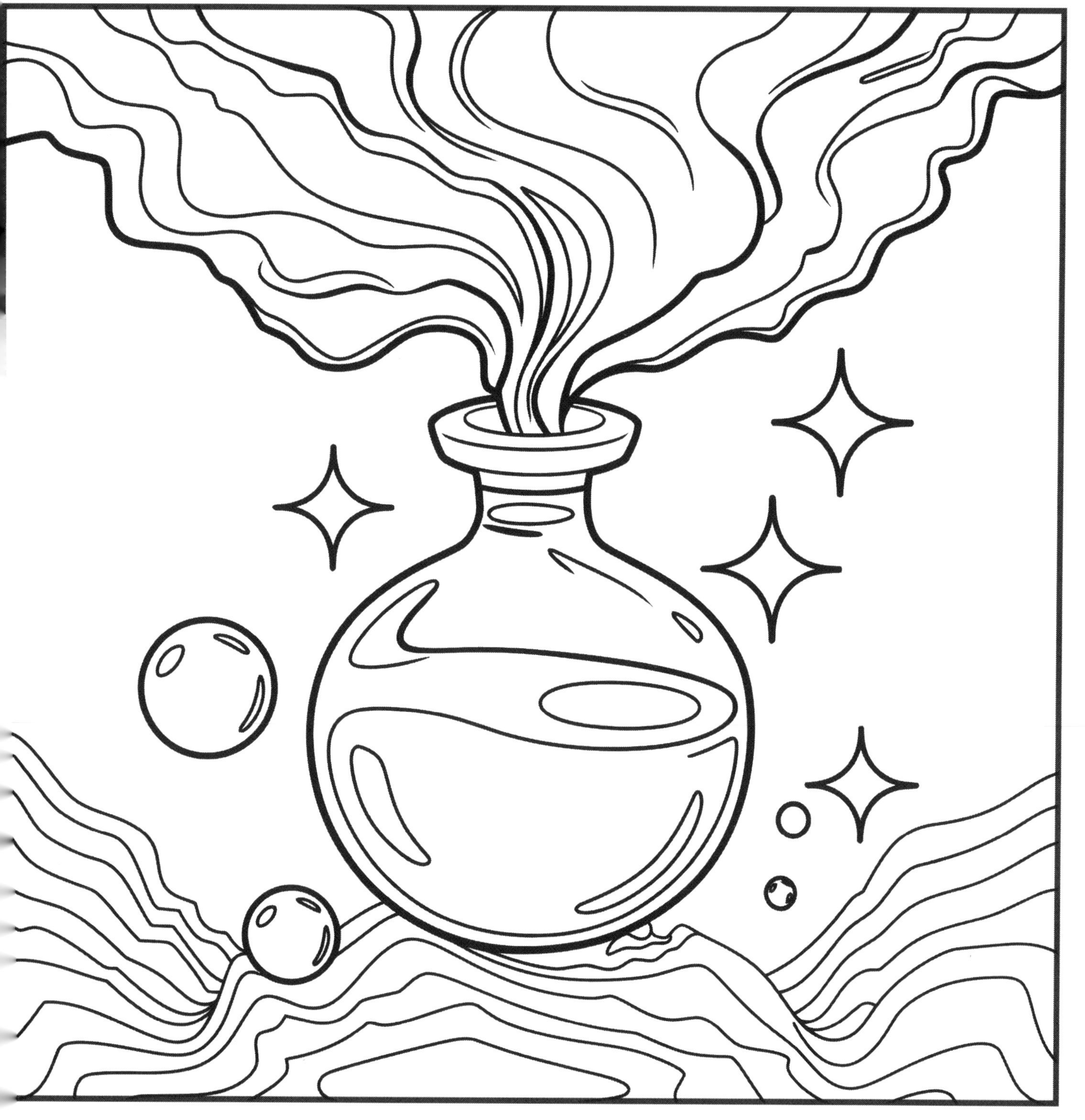

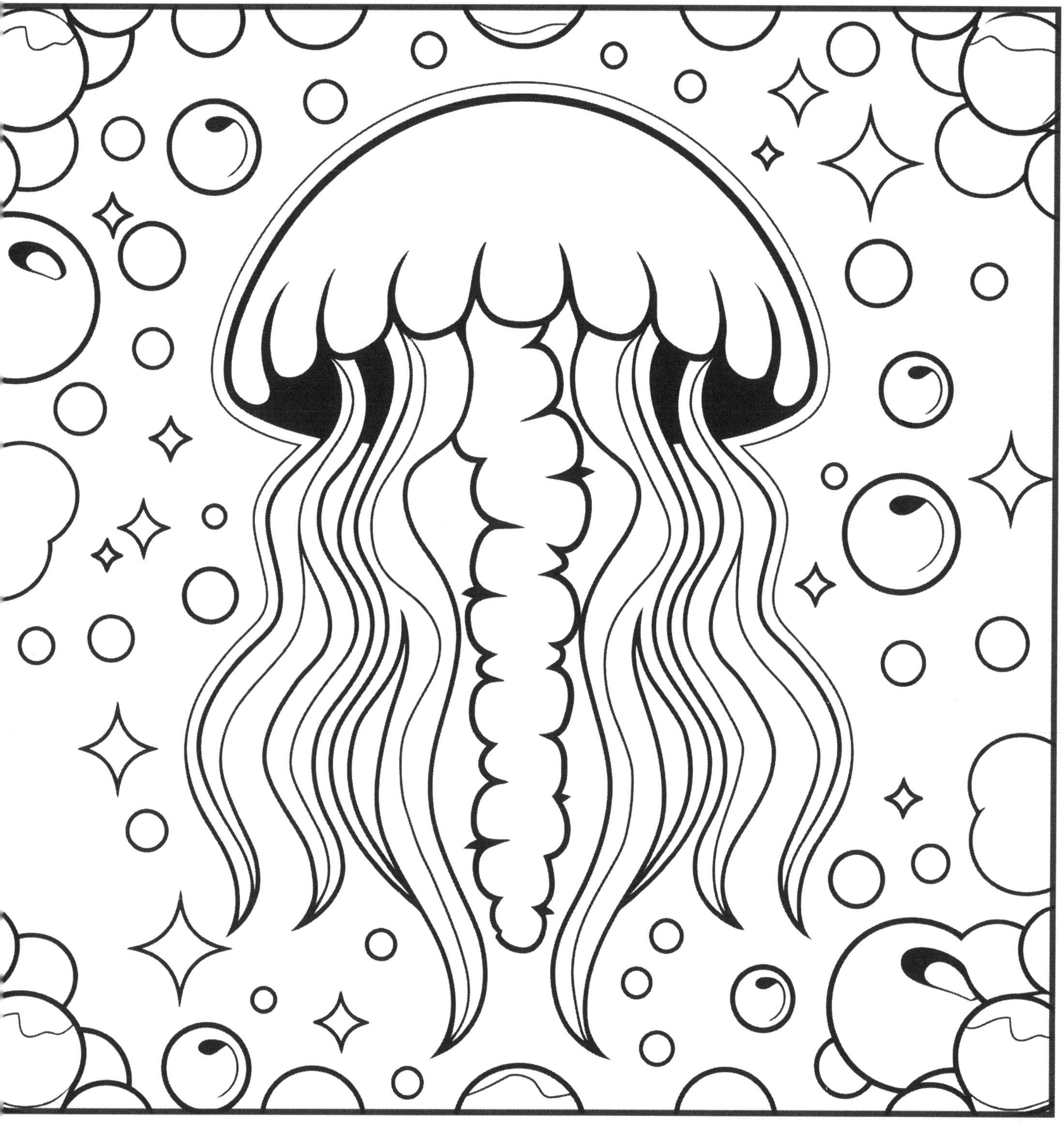

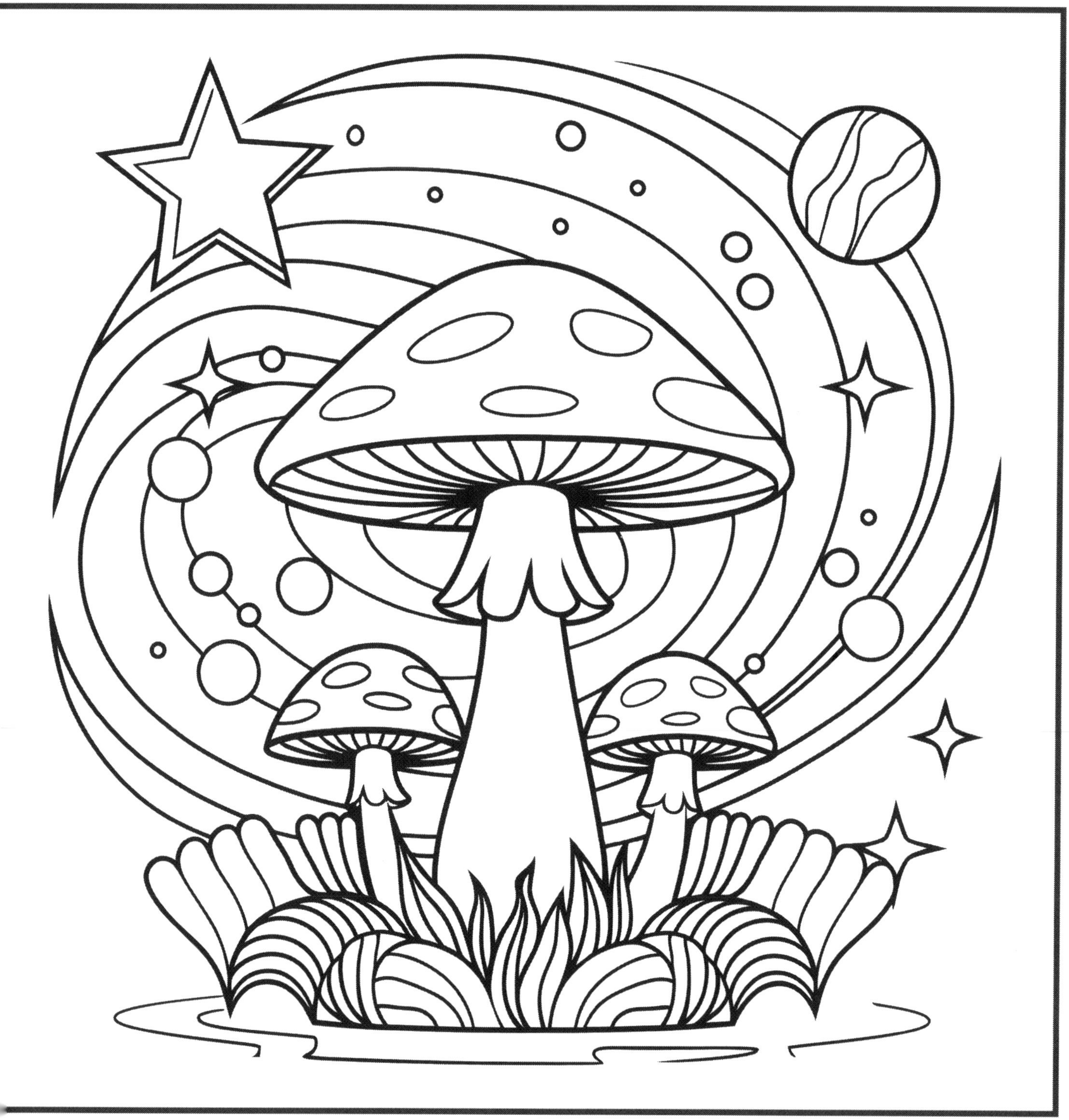

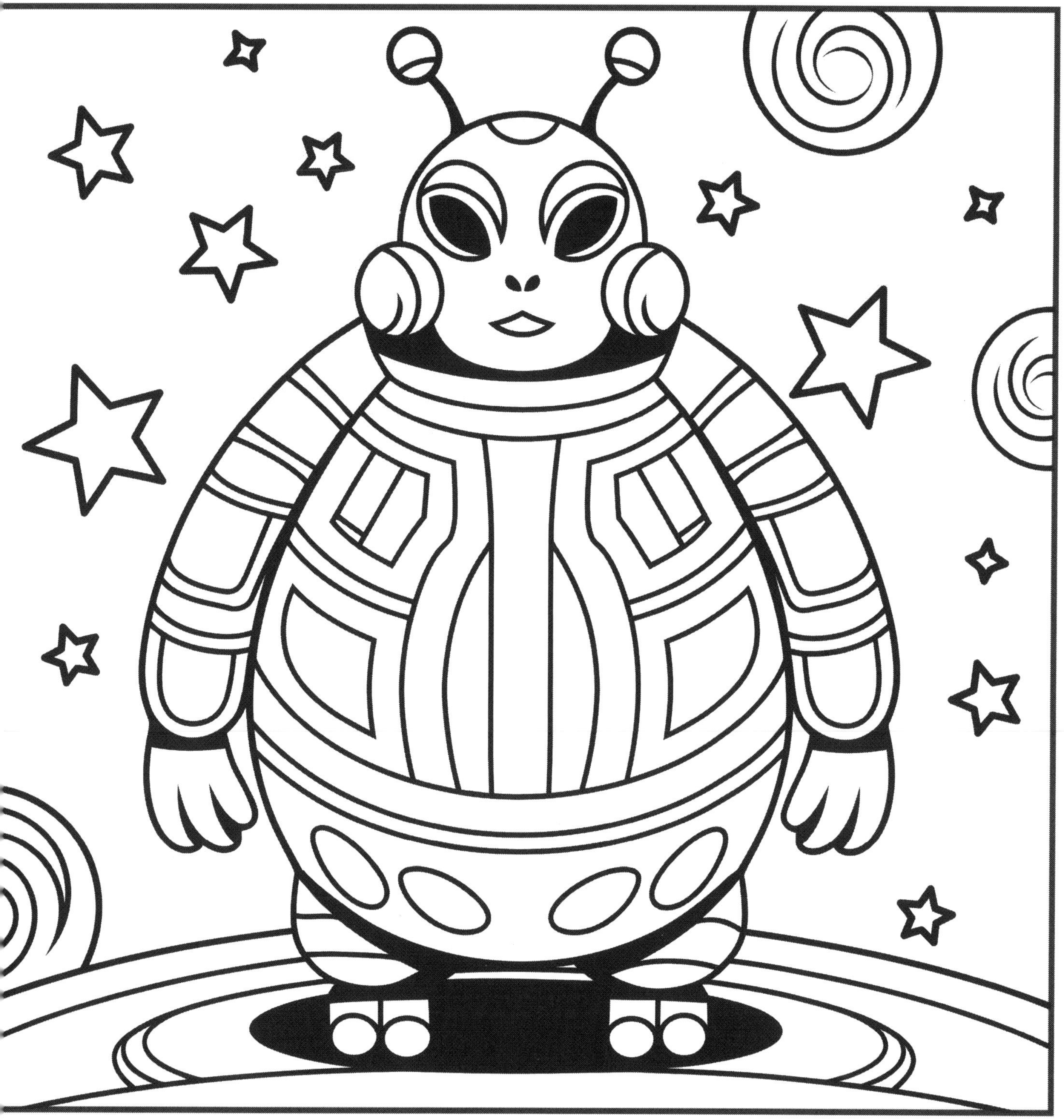

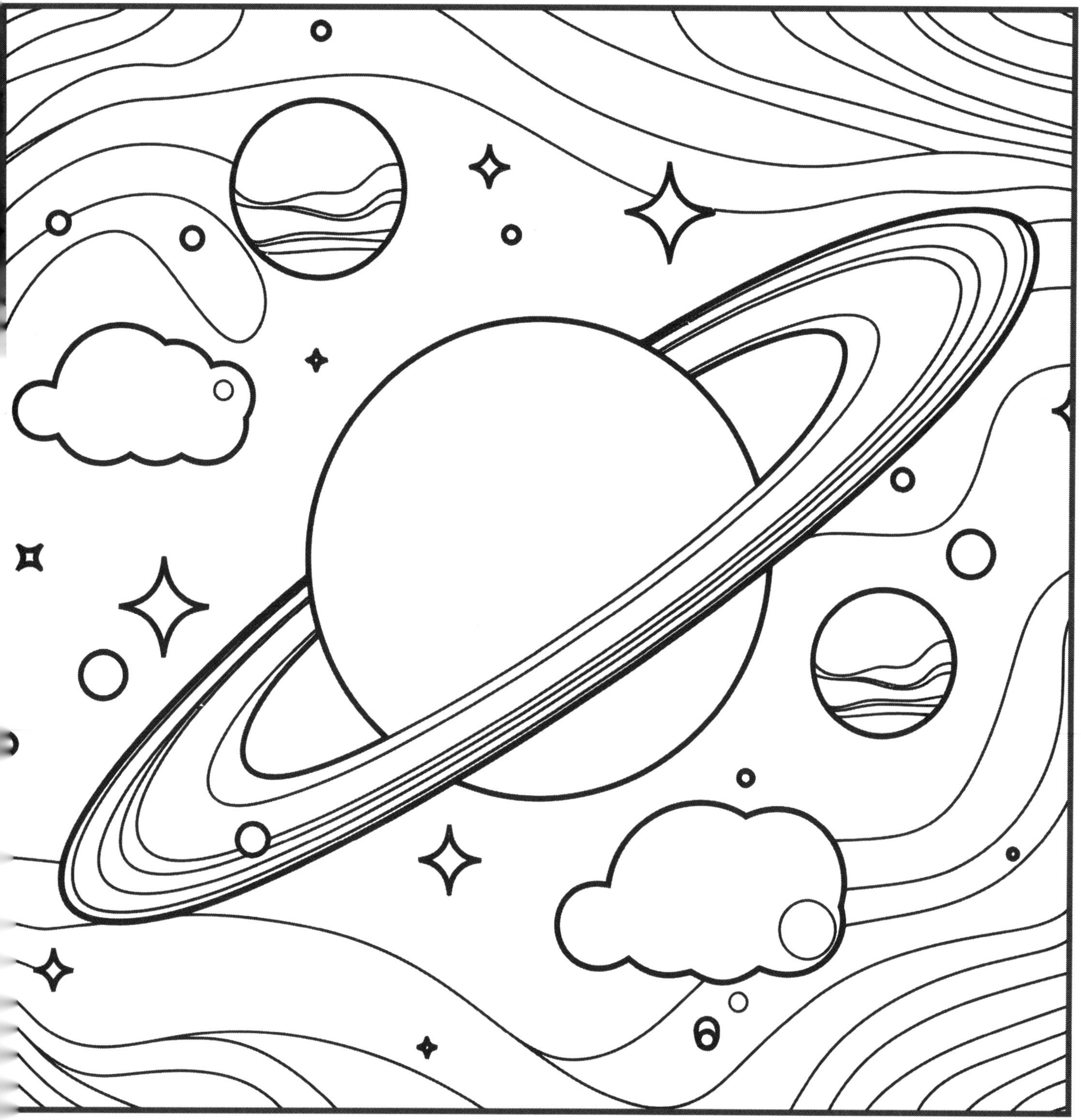

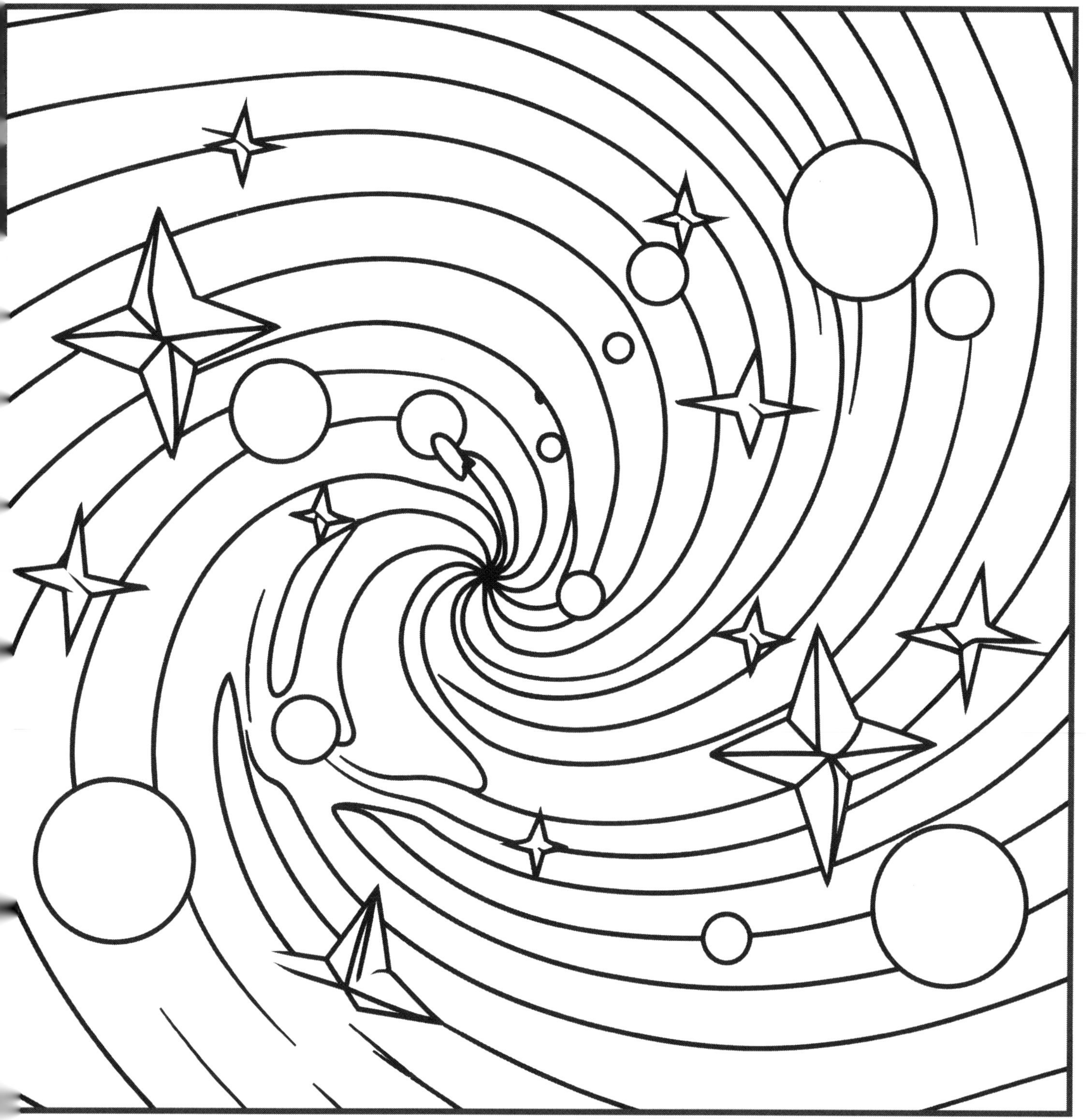

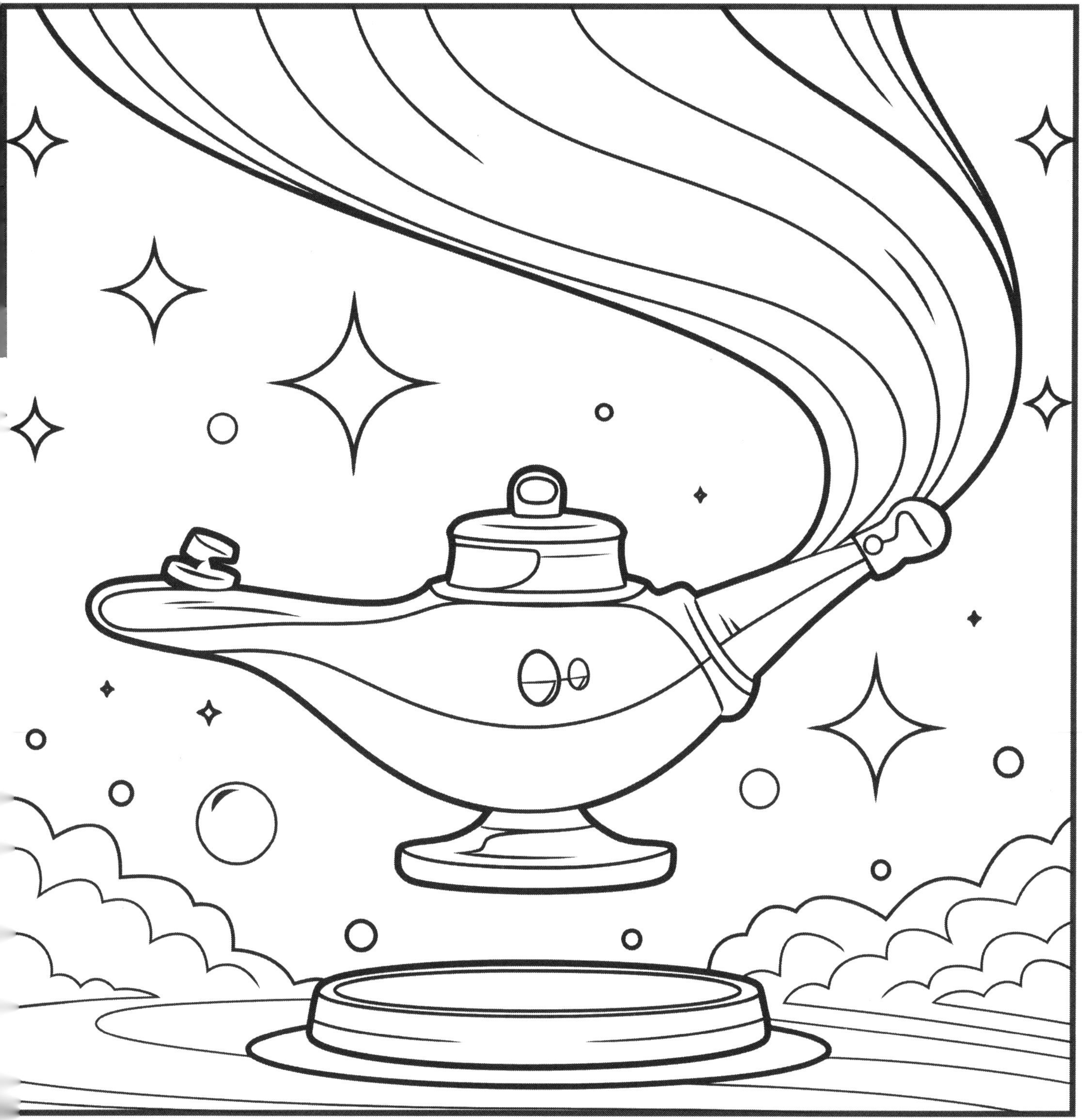

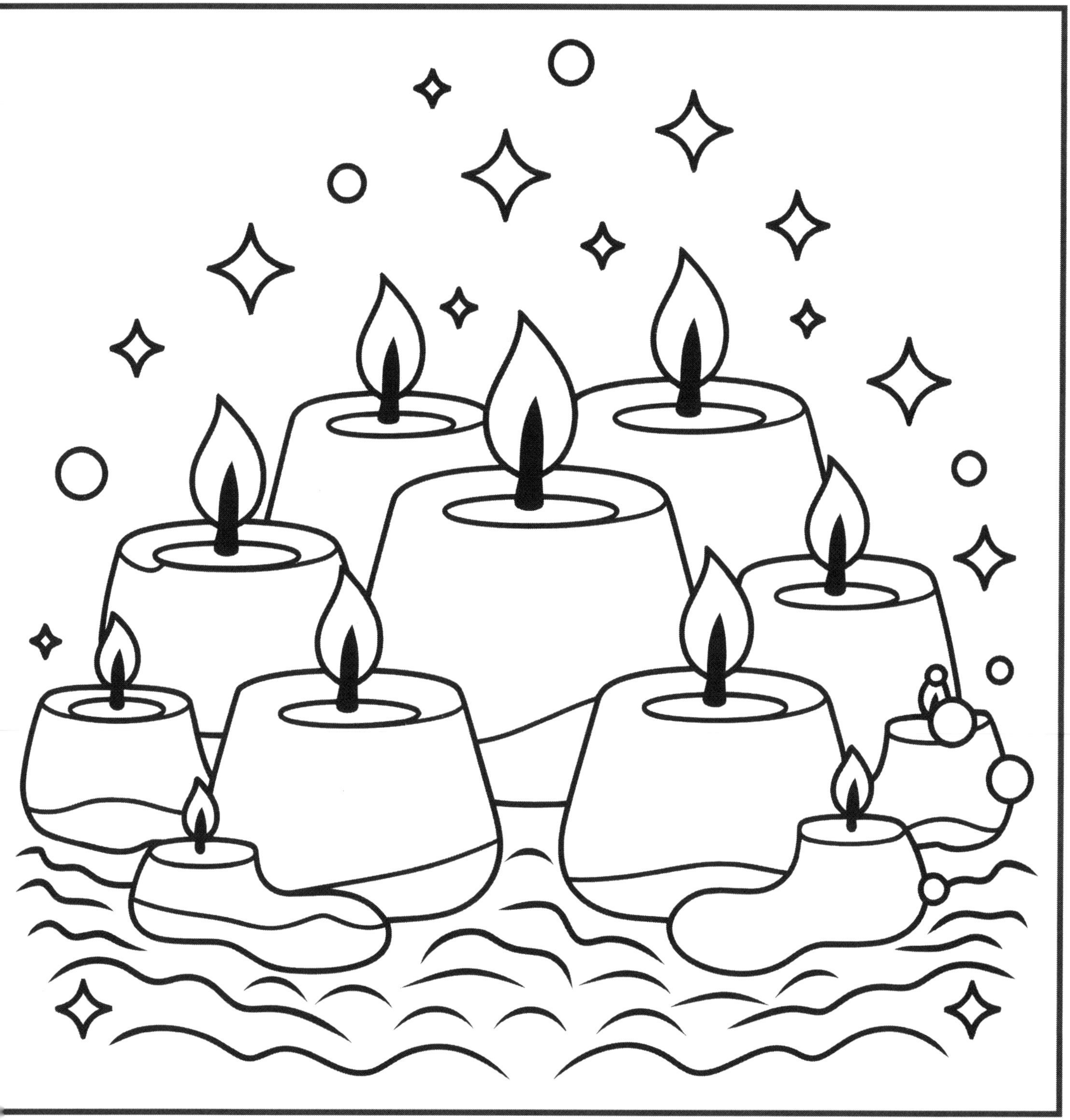

Made in United States
Orlando, FL
02 December 2024

54799971R00057